Jadwiga Smith, Anna Kapusta

Writing Life

Suffering as a Poetic Strategy of Emily Dickinson

Jagiellonian
University Press

The publication of this volume was supported by the Jagiellonian University – Faculty of Polish Studies

Reviewer
prof. dr hab. Beata Szymańska

Cover designer
Anna Sadowska
Cover graphic art, entitled *Light (2011)*, was prepared by Anna Kapusta

ISBN 978-83-233-3260-2

www.wuj.pl

Jagiellonian University Press
Editorial Offices:
Michałowskiego St. 9/2, 31-126 Cracow
Phone: +48 12 631 18 81, +48 12 631 18 82, Fax: +48 12 631 18 83
Distribution:
Phone: +48 12 631 01 97, Fax: +48 12 631 01 98
Cell Phone: +48 506 006 674, e-mail: sprzedaz@wuj.pl
Bank Account: PEKAO SA, IBAN PL80 1240 4722 1111 0000 4856 3325

Table of Contents

Acknowledgements

This book has been published with the assistance of a grant obtained from the Faculty of Polish Studies of the Jagiellonian University. The authors wish to express their gratitude to the Dean of the Polish Faculty Prof. dr hab. Jacek Popiel. For Their various support we would like to show our appreciation to: Prof. dr hab. Ryszard Nycz, Prof. dr hab. Mariola Flis, Dr Ewa Panecka and Dr Tomasz Sikora. We also wish to thank Prof. dr hab. Beata Szymańska for Her kindness, involvement, invaluable suggestions and recommendation of our work for publication. Finally we are indebted to Tony Ames for language consultation and His patient copyediting of the final text. Without These People this book would not have been possible.

The authors of this book

Introduction

The Martyr Poets – did not tell –
But wrought their Pangs in syllable –
That when their mortal name be numb –
Their mortal fate – encourage Some
(Dickinson 265)

Suffering is one of those taboo words that people prefer to avoid, perhaps because it is associated with weakness and defeat. Yet, it is the most universal feeling inextricably connected with human existence. Emily Dickinson is among those poets who confronted pain and gave it a new meaning. Living the life of a recluse the poet concentrated on her intensive inner life using her anxieties and personal transcendence as the subject matter of her poems. Translation of her painful experiences into a metaphor resulted in the most vivid and original verse. Recognizing the healing power of poetry Dickinson used it as self-therapy and reached out to all those gripped by pain. In one of her letters she wrote: "My business is to love" and "My business is to sing" (Dickinson, Todd 146).

The poet's biggest achievement as a consoler was to demonstrate the dualistic nature of suffering. She showed that on the one hand pain acts as a dispiriting factor which deprives us of motivation and reduces us to our physical nature, but on the other it can elevate us spiritually and lead to a more profound perception of life. In her exploration of the complexity of pain she emphasizes its central position in life. The common observation the poet makes in her work is that while pleasure is occasional, suffering is more widespread and felt with greater intensity. While grieving over losses and lamenting the transient character of things she showed feelings of agony acute enough to stifle vitality and drain the spirit. However, in many poems, she points to the fact that without suffering there would be no experience of delight. Just as a blind man learns of the existence of the sun, we should learn to recognize suffering as crucial for experiencing joy and elation. Sorrow, by bringing intensification of experience, gives better insight into the true nature of things and thus can be a way to raise oneself above the commonplace. In many poems the poet celebrates the power to transcend one's vulnerability and rise beyond suffering (Scheurich 195).

The critical tool chosen for the analysis of Emily Dickinson's poetry is the work of Julia Kristeva as her theory explains the function of pain in human biography. She refers to the earliest and most universal anthropological experience of every person, namely, being a part of a mother's body. According to Kristeva the primary painful event in everyone's life is separation from the maternal body and the first signal of human suffering is the cry of a new-born baby, who feels brutally separated from the comfort and safety of the mother's womb. Speech is also a result of this imposed deprivation: "'lack' is necessary for the *sign* to emerge" (Kristeva 23). Applying Kristeva's theory to Emily Dickinson's poetry reveals that at the centre of Dickinson's poetic texts is an oscillation between the desire for the mother's presence and the necessity of separation from her. This is the general definition of suffering that the poet formulates. This work concentrates on the tension between the biographical deficiencies and the compulsive need for creation. Emily Dickinson is a poet of such tension caused by suffering and necessity to write. Therefore we can say that suffering became her poetic strategy.

In the two following chapters of this thesis an attempt will be made to prove that personal anguish moulded the three major components of the poet's work: the theme, the language, and the form. All of these aspects are integral parts of a literary work in the theory of Julia Kristeva. The dualistic nature of suffering parallels with her theory of a double dimension of the text – the semiotic reflects suffering as the destructive and depressive state while the symbolic its successful overcoming.

In her literary criticism Julia Kristeva concentrates on the role of the author and regards the writer as a crucial element in the interpretation of a text. The critic links psychological processes to literature through various channels such as the relationship between suffering and creativity, the limits of language and the acquisition of the symbolic order. According to Kristeva we are all "subjects-in-process" (qtd. in McAfee 69) representing the struggle between bodily drives and their successful conquest. Chapter One of this thesis investigates Emily Dickinson's quest for subjectivity – her wrestling with the repressed desires undermining the autonomous self.

The first part of Chapter One – "Suffering as a dispiriting factor" – focuses on suffering as the central feature in the representation of emotional deprivation, unfulfilled love and her ambivalent relationship to God. Many poems are studied to illustrate the metaphorisation of the poet's poor physical conditions and psychic distress. Emily Dickinson's poetry is not confessional, individual persons or circumstances are never mentioned in the verse, yet, personal motifs can be easily discovered behind her poetic images. Activated by a life of withdrawal her *dispiriting* poems are metaphors of denial and sorrow.

The second part – "The Empowering side of suffering" – demonstrates the compensatory rewards of pain. Emily Dickinson's ideas about the creative power of suffering helped her to transform her life of isolation and anxiety into poetic texts. In the *empowering* poems she celebrates immortality and liberation from conventions. Sorrow is changed into a constructive defiance and an assertive and exuberant mood dominates the texts. The powerful voice of the poems signifies the overcoming of suffering and a victorious self-transcendence.

The prerequisite for creation is a successful separation from the maternal body. Chapter Two introduces Julia Kristeva's theory of abjection and the semiotic and symbolic energies. These theories are presented in their relation to Emily Dickinson's poems in three parts. The first one: "Julia Kristeva's theory of abjection in Emily Dickinson's poetry" – gives an outline of the concept of abjection – a primary psychological force of rejection of the mother-figure. An attempt is made to illustrate the extent to which Kristeva's ideas are applicable to Dickinson's poetry and how the *way* from the first experience of loss to the completion of mourning found its reflection in her poems.

Part two of this chapter: "The semiotic features in Emily Dickinson's poetic language," is devoted to linguistic representation of suffering in the poetry of Dickinson. As language cannot function in the world of isolation, Julia Kristeva draws a close analogy between language and the author's state of mind. Although semiotic energies do not signify, they communicate as much as the symbolic. Therefore they cannot be ignored during interpretation of the literary text. Emily Dickinson's style of writing discloses a rich semiotic imagination, which means that the maternal energies most of the time outweigh the symbolic. That is what makes her poetic texts hermetic and difficult to interpret.

While analysing Holbein's painting in *Black Sun* Julia Kristeva poses the question: "Can Disenchantment Be Beautiful?" (126). Her contemplation of whether the truth, which is "severe, sometimes sad, often melancholy" (127), constitutes beauty ends in the affirmative. This conclusion points to the aesthetic function of suffering, which can be used for conquering its destructive side. The third part of the second chapter concentrates on the poetic strategies of Emily Dickinson and her techniques for depicting suffering.The objective is to present the creative aspect of Emily Dickinson's writing. Through what Kristeva calls "unbelievable symbolic effort" (qtd. in Mills 94) mourning is transformed into a sublimatory activity, which "transposes affect into rhythms, signs, forms. The 'semiotic' and the 'symbolic' become communicable imprints of an affective reality" (Kristeva 22). As the symbolic element is present in all of the strategies, this section of the thesis is devoted to the symbolic dimension of Emily Dickinson's poetry.

Chapter 1
The Dualistic Nature of Suffering

Chapter One focuses on suffering as the theme of Emily Dickinson's poems. It presents the dualistic nature of suffering – the dispiriting and empowering side – which the poet illustrated in her verse. Following Julia Kristeva's concept that *lack* is a starting point for the creative process, four types of lack, which became the basis for the most agonising poems, have been distinguished: lack of maternal love, lack of romantic love, lack of God and lack of health. Juxtaposed in the second section are the compensatory, rewarding aspects of suffering: the concept of immortality, an unorthodox feminine role, rage as a constructive factor and the new spirituality. The process of thought transformation denotes the poet's healing process or using Kristeva's term a successful mourning for the lost Thing.

1.1. Suffering as a dispiriting factor

> She walked this life... with the firm
> step of martyrs who sing while
> they suffer... (qtd. in Farr 13)

When we come into contact with great art we often ask ourselves questions about its origin; what inspired the genius, where did the energy that sustained years-long effort come from. Gabora and Holmes in their essay *Reflection on the Creative Writing Process* contemplate the connection between suffering and art. They observe that what differentiates creative individuals is their sensitivity which often ensures suffering and the tendency to emotional instability. Critics tend to disregard the biographical pressure that compels inventive creation and so do the artists who prefer saying that their work is independent from personal experiences, however the fact remains that they often tap into their memories and draw widely from the riches and pain that have accumulated for years (4).

Most critics agree that it was deficiency and mental torment that inspired Emily Dickinson's work. John Cody made an observation that the poet "never cited a zest for living, a sense of ecstasy, or a feeling of fulfilment as the springboards of her creative outpouring" (490). Although he seems to be convinced that the poet wrote to ease her pain, he also mentions "she had learned that she could suffer fruitfully, extracting artistic gains from deprivation" (496). What is more he postulates that there would be no Emily Dickinson's poetry but for the pain and deprivation she experienced (496). This assertion is in accord with the result of McDermott's research, which examined periods of Emily Dickinson's productivity and found a close connection between the poet's emotional crisis and her augmented output. The bulk of her poetry was written between the years 1862–1865 just after the time she herself refers to as "the Terror." In a letter to Thomas Higginson she writes: "Terror - since September – I could tell none – and so I sing, as the Boy does by the Burying Ground – because I am afraid –" (qtd. in McDermott 5–6). Richard Swell also attributes Emily Dickinson's art to her life of deprivation (Porter 2), and Adrienne Rich declares that, recognizing her creative ability, the poet purposefully chose a life of solitude to survive through poetry and to seek fulfilment in artistic expression (Porter 119).

Also Emily Dickinson admits herself that her poetry arose from distress and anguish. In a letter to Higginson she confessed that she "knew no tutor but the North" (qtd. in Cody 490). The North was the poet's symbol for suffering and great sadness. Not less explicit is she in poem 442 where she says: "The Tyrian would not come / Until the North- invoke it" (Dickinson 212). Tyrian – the royal purple colour – symbolizes poetry (Cody 490). The poet also tells us a lot about her strategy of writing. In poem 773 she refers to her life in isolation and says: "Deprived of other Banquet, I entertained Myself" (Dickinson 377). From poem 850 we find out that she wrote in the most difficult moments for her. The opening line starts with the words: "I sing to use the Waiting" and the poem closes "To keep the Dark away" (408). Emily Dickinson discloses here her depressive symptoms such as fear and anxiety and confesses that writing was part of her struggle with them – it kept her senses sound. Writing became a register of her self-exploration and examination: "I write to drive the awe away, yet awe impels the work" (qtd. in Cody 491). Although poetry was also her ambition, which she acknowledged saying "My business is to sing" (qtd. in Doriani 3), sorrow remained the main feature of her verse. She "sang off charnel steps" (qtd. in Cody 490).

Emily Dickinson's poetry reveals a strong connection between biographical fact and its metaphorical equivalent. One can virtually define her creative process as a way from biographical lack to its poetic expression in a text. In Julia Kristeva's theory deprivation stimulates imagination. Consequently, negative emotions become a spring of creativity. Suffering is transformed into phantasies which are later used as a tool in the process of creation. This section of the thesis will look at Emily Dickinson's biographical deficiencies and show how lack has triggered her productivity.

1.1.1. Lack of love

> Affection is like bread, unnoticed till we starve, and then we dream of it and sing of it and paint it. (qtd. in Cody 39)

One of the most painful factors which determined Emily's life was lack of love. She suffered from it during her infancy, childhood and in her adult life. All her life was a desperate attempt to fill the emotional vacuum which lovelessness created. She looked for affection at home, among her friends and suitors but the intense sense of solitude never left her. The significance she attaches to love can be easily recognized by noticing that the poet uses in her work the vocabulary of nourishment to talk about the emotional deficiency. The message seems clear – love like food is indispensable for survival (Cody 39). The following citations from her letters leave no doubt that the poet associates hunger and thirst with love. In a letter to her cousins who looked after her during her eye treatment she expresses her concern: "Do you find plenty of food at home? Famine is unpleasant" (qtd. in Cody 43). Years later when writing to her friend she observes: "Am told that fasting gives to food marvellous Aroma, but by birth a Bachelor, disavow Cuisine" (43). With time she found out that longing was a part of existence and sometimes more precious than fulfilment. Gratification was negative as it put an end to desires and led to shallowness of perception. She declined Judge Otis P. Lord's proposal of marriage saying: "It is Anguish I long conceal from you to let you leave me, hungry, but you ask the divine Crust and that would doom the Bread" (43). But while short refraining from eating enhances appetite waiting for years leads to emotional impairment and psychological imbalance.

That Emily Dickinson suffered from lovelessness is conspicuous in a gamut of poems. These poems would have probably never been written had it not been for the overpowering longing for affection. A very sad line opens poem 579: "I had been hungry, all the Years." The poet not only confesses her solitude which lasted for years but also reveals the ravenous craving for love. In the second stanza she continues:

> I did not know the ample Bread –
> 'T was so unlike the Crumb
> The Birds and I, had often shared
> in Nature's – Dining Room – (Dickinson 283)

The deprivation seemed so painful that the poet was not free from envy as in the previous stanza she admits:

> When turning, hungry, Home
> I looked in Windows, for the Wealth
> I could not hope – for Mine – (283)

The same theme of insufficiency, expressed in terms of drink, runs through poem 132, which starts with the lines "I bring an unaccustomed wine / To lips long parching" and continues "If, haply, mine may be the drop" (62). The last line indicates that the poet almost came to terms with the deficiency and stopped expecting more, however, not without a feeling of bitterness and disappointment.

Sounding almost like an extension of this poem is another one "Come slowly – Eden! / Lips unused to Thee –" (Dickinson 98). The scarcity brought with itself the sense of unfamiliarity and subsequent caution. Something that happens on such rare occasions becomes so precious that one is not capable of enjoying it fully for fear of doing something wrong and ruining it. But, even though fearful, the new experiences always taste the best. Poem 1125 gives proof of this claim "Oh Sumptuous moment / Slower go / That I may gloat on thee –" (505) The poet wants to hold on to the moment of happiness, wants it to pass as slowly as possible so that she can rejoice in the bliss. She knows, however, that the ecstasy will only be followed by craving for more: "T'will never be the same to starve / Now I abundance see" (505). Sometimes it is better to live in ignorance and not to know what delights and pleasures life has to offer. Having a morsel when one starves only increases one's desire.

In poem 460 the old attentiveness is forgotten and the speaker is ready to quench her thirst with buckets. In the third stanza we read: "Were I rich / A bucket I would buy – / I'm often thirsty –" (Dickinson 221). But the buckets seem to be reserved only for the fortunate ones and perhaps belong more to literature than reality, as further on we find out:

> I read in an Old fashioned Book
> That People "thirst no more" –
> The Wells have Buckets to them there –
> It must mean that – I'm sure – (Dickinson 221)

The capitalized and separated adjective "Old" may mean that the abundance is a thing of the past. Still the image of wells with buckets contrasts drastically with the word "thirsty" from the previous stanza.

How difficult it is to remain thirsty while knowing the satisfying quality of water became a theme of poem 490.

> To One denied to drink
> To tell what Water is
> Would be acuter, would it not
> Than letting Him surmise?
>
> To lead Him to the Well
> And let Him hear it drip
> Remind Him, would it not, somewhat
> Of His condemned lip? (Dickinson 235)

The poet seems to make a point that true loneliness is not yearning for something unknown, undefined but it comes with longing for something one has lost or something that was within the reach, yet still unattainable.

A tone of hopelessness permeates poem 612 where the poet finds herself more disadvantaged than a biting fly, which at least has the chance to look for nourishment.

> Nor like the Gnat – had I –
> The privilege to fly
> And seek a Dinner for myself –
> How mightier He – than I – (Dickinson 301)

Birds too are more favoured by God as he was more generous with them "God gave a loaf to every Bird – / But just a Crumb to Me –" (386). Sometimes the longing for love seemed unbearable and she lamented her lot with strong words as in poem 801 "Too hungry to be borne" (391).

1.1.2. Lack of maternal love

> The child king becomes irredeemably sad before uttering his first words; this is because he has been irrevocably, desperately separated from the mother, a loss that causes him to try to find her again, along with other objects of love, first in the imagination, than in words (Kristeva 6).

The first source of love is always the mother; however, the poet's relationship with her mother was far from close. Although they spent their life in the same house, and looked after each other, there was neither emotional nor spiritual bond. Emily Norcross, even if well intentioned, proved to be an inadequate mother, struggling with her own depression and hypochondria. The poet viewed her mother as shy, submissive woman who "does not care for thought" and whose faculties are "unobtrusive" (qtd. in Cody 94). All three children sought comfort from each other (40). The most trenchant criticism Emily expressed in words "I never had a mother" (qtd. in Wolff 45) and in a letter to Higginson "I always ran Home to Awe as a child, if anything befell me. He was an awful Mother, but I liked him more than none" (45).

Cody interprets Poem 959 as the voice of a child longing for something that is gone. The grief seems to result from an emotional impoverishment and thus the critic guesses it is a cry for affection from an incompetent mother.

> A loss of something ever felt –
> The first that I could recollect
> Bereft I was – of what I knew not
> Too young that any should suspect (Dickinson 448)

In poem 612 the poet candidly admits her longing for emotional intimacy, and the use of the word "child" intensifies the degree of unfulfilled desire for love.

> It would have starved a Gnat –
> To live so small as I –
> And yet I was a living Child –
> With Food's necessity (Dickinson 301)

Emily Dickinson was not rejected by her mother in the literal sense of this word, but what really lacked in their relationship was communication. Cynthia Griffin Wolff characterises Emily Norcross as an affectionate but silent and unresponsive woman who "communicated her wishes indirectly, through a complex and often inefficient game of verbal hide-and-sick" (39). The authors of *Triple Takes on Curricular Worlds* propose that it was this lack of verbal interaction with her mother that shaped Emily Dickinson's poetic strategy.

> When critics write of Dickinson's minimalism – the power of words as well as their limitations, her cryptic use of language, the slant of her rhymes – they are actually noting how Dickinson gives voice to the silences of her mother tongue. Literally. By withholding, by using suggestions, by not filling in the gaps of meaning, Emily writes in such a radically different way that she depaternalizes the notion of authority, elevating instead the realm of the unsaid (Doll, Wear, Whitaker 157).

Inadequate maternal care also influenced Emily Dickinson's outlook on the world. The fear which underlies so many of her poems derives from her perception of the world as hostile and unloving. In a letter to Jane Humphrey she writes: "How lonely the world is growing, something so desolate creeps over the spirit and we don't know its name, and it won't go away" (qtd. in Mamunes 52). Although she refers mostly to God, lack of faith alone would not create such misery. The words point to emotional deprivation and solitude.

John Cody suggests that in her desperate quest for love she tried to find a surrogate mother in such women as Mrs J. Holland, Sue, and her aunt Lavinia. In a letter to Mrs Holland she writes: "Love me if you will, for I had rather *be* loved than to be called a king in earth, or a lord in Heaven" (qtd. in Cody 123). Strong hunger for Sue's affection finds its manifestation in a letter to her in which Emily writes: "Oh Susie, I would nestle close to your warm heart, and never hear the wind blow, or the storm beat again. Is there any room for me, or shall I wander away all homeless and alone" (qtd. in Cody 216). In these words Emily sounds like an insecure child seeking safety at the side of her mother (216).

John Cody also finds lots of allusions to unresolved emotions from childhood in Emily's poetry. He suggests that expressions like "Bliss" and "Murder" in poem 379 and "Had I a mighty gun / I think I'd shoot the human race" in poem 118 indicate a dormant fury which originated in her early days and was caused by rejection by her mother (363).

1.1.3. Lack of romantic love

> Depressive person cannot endure Eros, they prefer to be with the Thing up to the limit of negative narcissism leading them to Thanatos. They are defended against Eros by sorrow but without defense against Thanatos because they are wholeheartedly tied to the Thing. Messengers of Thanatos, melancholy people are witness/accomplices of signifier's flimsiness, the living being's precariousness (Kristeva 20).

In Emily's letters there are several men mentioned that she may have had crushes on. It is difficult to decide whether in her poetry and letters Emily Dickinson describes actual events or if these were just her fantasies. However the multiple metaphors in her work and letters is proof that Emily Dickinson was a woman full of suppressed desires and not as ascetic as her secluded and solitary life would imply (Wolff 136). However, her longing made her look at love as something very precious but also fragile, evasive, scary and more associated with pain than happiness. Even while dreaming of it she did not idealize it, she did not describe the passion, ecstasy and bliss that happy lovers extol. Instead Dickinson paints a picture of love fraught with difficulties, disappointment and uncertainty. Over and over again the pattern of disenchantment appears in her poems and the verse speaks with anguish (136). A very common theme of Dickinson's love poetry is that the lovers are not able to be together, hindered by some unknown power. They are devoted to each other and tied by a profound love, yet cannot be united. But Wolff makes an interesting observation "If lovers could be together there would be no poetry" (416). It is the painful loss that triggered Emily Dickinson's poetry and the aching separation evoked feelings that compelled immortalization in verse. Even though her love poetry can sometimes be mischievous and light-hearted, it is the sense of lack of fulfilment that prevails in most of her work (416).

In poem 474 the lovers are separated by a distance as big as a sea. The speaker complains: "They put Us far apart– / As separate as Sea" (Dickinson 228). The lovers are forced to live without seeing each other: "They took away our Eyes– / They thwarted Us with Guns –" But distance only makes the yearning stronger and reinforces the tender feelings, so that, even if not personal, the lovers sustain some spiritual communication: "'I see Thee' each responded straight / Through Telegraphic Signs –" (228). The sea also separates lovers in the poem 249. The first stanza by the use of the subjunctive tense introduces the world of fantasy as the speaker romanticises what it would be like if they could be together (Vendler, *Dickinson: Selected Poems and Commentaries* 94).

Wild Nights – Wild Nights!
Were I with thee
Wild Nights should be
Our luxury! (Dickinson 114)

As the old meaning of the word "luxury" is lust and indulgence, the lover must be dreaming of unrestrained passion (Vendler 94). The desire is so overwhelming and powerful that no winds can hamper the lover on his or her way to the loved one. No compass is needed or a map, the sexual craving is enough to find the right direction. The last stanza emphasises the hypothesis of sexual intercourse as the speaker finishes the poem with the words:

Rowing in Eden –
Ah, the Sea!
Might I but moor – Tonight –
In Thee! (Dickinson 114)

Commenting on the sea symbol Leiter observes: "While the sea can symbolize many things in Dickinson's writing – freedom, wilderness, immortality, salvation – here it is surely what Farr calls 'an image of primal – sexual – waters'" (232). Emily Dickinson reveals herself in this poem as a very passionate woman.

The sea symbol appears again in poem 498 and although not separating the lovers it emphasizes the remoteness between them. Obsessive longing, apart from pain, also brought a feeling of envy, envy directed not only towards people but also nature and even physical objects.

I envy Seas, whereon He rides –
I envy Spokes of wheels
Of Chariots, that Him convey –
I envy Crooked Hills (Dickinson 241)

The constant, obstinate repetition betrays the despair of the speaker who longs to be where the lover is, yet for some undefined reason it is not possible. It seems as if an external force prohibited the happiness: "What is forbidden utterly / As Heaven – unto me!" (241). By comparing the impossible unification to "Heaven" the poet lays emphasis on the profundity of love and suffering caused by separation.

An acute sense of loneliness oppresses the speaker in one of the most famous Dickinson's love poem 640. The poem starts with the lines: "I cannot live with You – / It would be Life –" (Dickinson 317) and finishes with a word "Despair." Leiter calls this poem a "litany of loss" (90) and points to "the half-bitter, half resigned quality found in so many Dickinson poems in which the speaker acknowledges hunger and deprivation as a primary condition of her existence" (90). Having analysed different states of being with her lover, the speaker rejects them all. She realizes that everyday life would bring damage to mutual feelings. Love is compared in this poem to a cup which, when it is new gives joy, but when old, it is fragile and easily broken. As the poem progresses and emotions compete with logic, the dark mood grows even stronger and sometimes it verges on hysteria. The speaker laments: "I could not die – with You – / For One must wait / To shut the Other's Gaze down –" and a bit later "or could I rise – with You – Because Your Face / Would put out Jesus'– That New Grace." In her desperate search for solution the speaker goes beyond mortality and contemplates unification after death but realizes that by glorifying and viewing her lover more perfect than Jesus she renders the notion futile as well. Heavy symbolism – the porcelain cup, the Sexton with his key, the vast ocean, and half-closed door – heightens the dreary reality of the speaker's loneliness. The last stanza brings the heart-breaking conclusion: "So We must meet apart – / You there –I– here – / With just the Door ajar." Dickinson's famous dashes seem to be of especially prominent importance in this poem, as they enhance the distance between lovers and make it visual and graphic.

The motif of a strong yearning for love but at the same time refraining from it, is also explicit in poem 609.

> I Years had been from Home
> And now before the Door
> I dare not enter, lest a Face
> I never saw before (Dickinson 299)

John Cody suggests that if we interpret the word "Home" as love here, then the rest of the verse we can understand as the poet's confession in which she admits that although she had felt desire for years, now that she has the chance of fulfilment she is too scared to use the opportunity. He deciphers the symbol "Face" as desire or arousal by taking into account Emily Dickinson's letter to Judge Lord in which she writes: "How could I long to give who never saw you nature Face" (qtd. in Cody 137) and her poem "My Life had stood – a loaded Gun," where the "Vesuvian face" stands for the poet's sensuality and desire. Thus according to Cody the poet is abstaining not only from love but also from "sexual gratification." The refraining does not come easily as longing for closeness for years made her extremely vulnerable. Her temptation is so strong that she is close to collapsing: "I fitted to the Latch / My hand, with trembling care / Lest back the awful Door should spring / and leave me in the Floor –". After display of such horror the reader is not surprised by the final decision: "Fled gasping from the House" (137).

1.1.4. Lack of God

> I have assumed depressed persons to be atheistic – deprived of meaning, deprived of values. For them, to fear or to ignore the Beyond would be self-deprecating. Nevertheless, although atheistic, those in despair are mystics – adhering to the preobject, not believing in Thou, but mute and steadfast devotees of their own inexpressible container. (Kristeva 14)

"Why does an all-powerful, all loving God permit so much unspeakable misery in the world – disease, natural disasters, war? Above all, why does he allow the innocent to suffer?" (Keane 2) Emily Dickinson, who lived at the time of momentous changes brought about by the theories of Darwin and Nietzsche, was bothered throughout her life by the question of God's existence and His true nature. She tried to understand the role He played in the natural and human world marked by violence and suffering. On the one hand her Christian heritage induced yearning and a search for God; on the other hand she challenged and denounced His cruelty. Although she never denied Him she rejected many of the tenets of her own faith and her religious standpoint was dominated by defiance, anger and pain. While all members of Emily Dickinson's family submitted to conversion she still had her doubts about trusting a God who seemed too detached from the sorrows of this life. Repeatedly, a "channel of dust" (Dickinson 512) nullified the soothing effect of "that religion / That doubts as frequently as it believes" (qtd. in Keane 2).

In poem 338 she declares "I know that He exists" (Dickinson 160). But instead of supporting this confident expression of faith in the following stanzas, the poet is besieged by misgivings and her certitude gradually fades. "Somewhere – in Silence / He has hid his rare life / From our gross eyes" (160). The speaker cannot catch a glimpse of God because He is hidden from our undeserving eyes. By juxtaposing the word "rare" with "gross" the poet accentuates the disparity between God's greatness and our unworthiness. The "Silence" He is concealed in also points out towards the distance He created between Himself and us. God has moved so far away that He cannot possibly hear us; neither can we perceive any sound of his existence. In the second stanza Emily Dickinson states, as Shakespeare does in "As You Like It," that life is "an instant's play" and people are just players (Rutledge).

'Tis an instant's play.
'Tis a fond Ambush –
Just to make Bliss
Earn her own surprise! (Dickinson 160)

Despite increasing uncertainty, there is still some optimism: just as in a game of "fond Ambush" there will be a "surprise" at the end, God will reveal His presence and the perspective of His kingdom will appear before us. The exclamation mark after "surprise" augments the significance of the gift God has prepared for us. But the desired trust does not stay for long. The mood drastically changes in the third stanza by introduction of the single word "But." What if the "play" is not a game but "piercing earnest"? Doubt, which was only subtly present earlier, now becomes disturbing. The effect of growing apprehension is achieved by the repetition of the word "should" and the heavy "g" and "t" sound which push through the poem: "Should the glee-glaze / In Death's stiff– stare –" In addition the alliteration of three "p"s upsets the softness of the first part of the poem characterized by "t"s and "s"s. Also adding to the distressing mood of the poem is the way in which some words in the third stanza rhyme with the previous ones. "Stare" / "rare" and "glee" / "He" are placed in different position as if to prevent any sort of peaceful pattern. As the weight of words alters and "play" and "Bliss" are followed by "earnest" and "stiff" the poem's tone changes from light-hearted to fearful. Although the words in the final stanza are formed like questions, the speaker does not expect any answers. The question marks have been substituted with exclamation points only to bring the concern to the point of panic. With hope abandoned, life appears to be a bad joke, not worth living in the light of impending death. And the perpetrator who demands it from us is responsible for this bad joke and our suffering (Rutledge).

Emily saw the cruelty of an uncaring God not only among people, but also in nature. Every year she observed God's destructive action upon the blossoming flowers in her garden. In her poems the "blossom" epitomizes beauty, joy and innocence, appreciated even more because of their transient qualities. Even though written in a tone of detached objectivity, poem 1624 evokes in the reader a strong emotional response as it portrays the decapitation of happy flowers by a merciless frost. It compels the reader to face the conflict between a benevolent God and a brutal natural world.

Apparently with no surprise
To any happy Flower
The frost beheads it as its play –
In accidental power –
The blonde Assassin passes on –
The Sun proceeds unmoved

To measure off another Day
For an Approving God (Dickinson 667).

The poem has no lyric "I" but the personal perspective is achieved by the introductory word "Apparently" as well as judgmental adjectives such as: "happy," "accidental" and "approving." Although the poet does not name her own emotions the strong vocabulary she uses – "beheads," "assassin," "unmoved Sun" – betrays her distress and helplessness. The tone verges on being submissive, angry, even blasphemous (Keane 26). The worst sort of crime is happening under the patronage of the all-powerful God. James McIntosh cites this poem as an example of Emily's endless concern with "God's heartless omnipotence" (46) and comments that as only we humans are capable of compassion and shock at the injustice of this world we are "lonely as well as bereft in the created universe" (47).

In an earlier poem 116 "I had some things that I called mine," which depicts a similar mutilation in the garden at God's command, the poet gets so upset that she threatens to take some legal "Action" and seek justice.

I'll institute an "Action" –
I'll vindicate the law –
Jove! Choose your counsel –
I'll retain "Shaw"! (Dickinson 55)

The last line "I'll retain Shaw" refers to Lemuel Shaw, chief justice of the Massachusetts Supreme Court from 1830 to 1860 (Keane 27). Emily Dickinson appears to be preparing her own defence in the highest court.

Emily Dickinson remained a seeker who was never comfortable in a world full of gratuitous suffering but also could not live without God. Though dismissive of all institutional churches and creeds she was drawn to preachers such as Edward Hale and Wadsworth (Keane 210) and was eager for religious experience. On some occasions she put aside her scepticism and ventured into religious certitude, but even such compromise on her side was not appreciated by the Almighty, who remained silent. Prayers occupy the central position of more than twenty poems, but while normally they increase one's intimacy with God, Emily Dickinson's poems reveal His absence, which becomes an immense source of the poet's pain. Poem 376 sounds like a bitter complaint. The speaker, in her suffering, seeks consolation from heaven, but her desperate appeal is met with total ignorance and indifference.

Of course – I prayed –
And did God Care?
He cared as much as on the Air
A Bird – had stamped her foot – (Dickinson 179)

Prayer that induces no response results in doubt and questioning the sense of life. It is as ineffective as a bird's stamping in the air. Life becomes a misery as the realization of being cheated gets stronger. With the words: "Life – / I had not had – but for Yourself –" the speaker blames the Creator. Although her life is due to His command, lifeless stones are more merciful than His "smart Misery." The consciousness He bestowed on us brings nothing but a painful awareness of being abandoned and left to oneself. In moments of real despair her prayers turned into combination of pleading and annoyance. In the opening line of poem 1076 the speaker almost hysterically implores for a sign: "Just Once! Oh least Request!" (Dickinson 488) but a moment later, getting impatient, she changes her tone: "Would not a God of Flint / Be conscious of a sigh?" (488) The "God of Flint" is probably the unyielding deity who stole so many dear ones from her and who could, unrestrained by any law cause so much devastation in her garden.

The question about His silence not only kept nagging the poet: "Our little secrets slink away – / Beside God's shall not tell –" (Dickinson 575) but instigated her anger. A world without a protective God is an alien place, in which one is like "The Drop that wrestles in the Sea –" and "forgets her own locality" (Dickinson 131). The "Drop," feeling completely lost and struggling in an intimidating universe, pleads for her identity in vain. Her appeals remain unanswered, because, as asserted in poem 358 "God is a distant – stately Lover" (Dickinson 170). The Drop's biggest torment is that of suspense, of the unknown, of anticipation of its own termination. The notion that "Suspense" is agonizing the poet is expressed in poem 705 "Suspense – is Hostiler than Death –" (Dickinson 347) and in poem 1331 "Wonder – is not precisely Knowing / And not precisely Knowing not," but "Suspense... is the Gnat that mangles men" (577). For the poet struggling with faith, the promise of eternity is not enough. She is terrified by the awareness of the inevitable end of existence and lack of any confirmation that God exists (Stiles 51–53).

Whilst living through an era of religious revolution, Dickinson contributed to it significantly. Taking into account her genius and the amount of poetry she produced, she can be positioned next to her contemporaries Herman, Melville, Fyodor Dostoevsky and Friedrich Nietzsche. Like them, she contemplated the loss of God and all its consequences. Although she did not dare to discard God's presence from her life, in the moments of her greatest doubts she was as fierce and blunt as any oath of Melville's Ahab or Nietzsche's Zarathustra (Lundin 151). In poem 1551 she maintains,

> Those – dying then,
> Knew where they went –
> They went to God's Right Hand –
> That hand is amputated now
> And God cannot be found (Dickinson 646).

The poem states that in the past it was much easier to believe. The dying went where the Apostles' message led them: "To God's Right Hand" – a hand of protection. But now that the hand is severed, we have no clue where to look for guidance (Lundin 151).

All the unanswered prayers, God's destructive qualities, his claim for the ones she loved led to the poet's growing resentment. Her associations with the Almighty became very painful. In the poem "There's a certain Slant of light" (Dickinson 118) the speaker says that "Cathedral Tunes" and winter afternoon light oppress her soul, giving her a "Heavenly Hurt." This pain causes no external scars but "internal difference" which suddenly renders the weightless light as heavy as the sound coming from massive church organs. The slanted light becomes a metaphor for existential despair that allows no relief as it is a "Seal Despair – / An imperial affliction" which is sent "of the Air." The despondency becomes so overwhelming that the whole "Landscape listens" and participates in her agony. Even when the depression lessens she is still powerless and it feels like "the Distance" has "the look of Death." She feels numb and isolated from herself. In his interpretation of the poem St. Armand writes that the light acts as a "penetrating spear" and that Dickinson suffers "internal scourging, crucifixion, and death, with no immediate hope for resurrection" (239).

Emily Dickinson wrestled with God and faith all her life. A few months before she died she called herself "Pugilist and Poet" (Lundin 4). Her relationship with God was one of love and hate. Although she was very blunt in addressing Him, and suffered enormously because of the contradictions she discovered, He was her closest companion. In poem 827 she admits "The Only One I meet/ Is God –" (Dickinson 401). Just like the biblical patriarch Jacob, who told the angel, "I will not let you go, unless you bless me" (Lundin 4), Dickinson did not let go of this very ambivalent relationship with the Almighty. The inconsistency between the faith she inherited and that which she intuited was a painful experience (4). In poem 1581 she noted "The abdication of Belief / Makes the Behaviour small" (Dickinson 646). God's love, protection and promise of eternity invigorate and give meaning to life whereas disbelief renders the spirit dry, as affirmed in poem 244.

> It is easy to work when the soul is at play –
> But when the soul is in pain –
> The hearing him put his playthings up
> Makes work difficult – then – (Dickinson 111)

Emily Dickinson never accepted the injustice and brutality of this world; neither did she approve of the omnipotent, merciless God, who seemed not to care about its own creation at all. She became closer to Jesus whom she saw as “a pioneer in the endless process of bearing pain” (Lundin 5) and the Transcendentalists who encouraged intuition rather than doctrines of established religions.

1.1.5. Lack of health

> Sorrow is the major outward sign that gives away the desperate person. Sadness leads us into that enigmatic realm of affects – anguish, fear, or joy. (Kristeva 22)

In accordance with Kristeva’s theory, as well as the opinion of James Guthrie, who noted that “illness or deformity modulate the register of expression” (4), three ailments are believed to have oppressed Emily Dickinson throughout her life – exotropia, agoraphobia and psychosis – will be examined and focused on through the eyes of some literary critics. In his book *Emily Dickinson’s Vision: Illness and Identity in her Poetry* James Guthrie asserts that eye problems were a key factor in Dickinson’s development as a poet. It was not only a formative experience for her but it also influenced her whole writing technique from observation to inscription. If we acknowledge that while writing poems Dickinson was ill and suffered severely, we can almost treat her output as a sort of personal diary of a battle against a serious disability. Illness always modifies the life of patients; it changes their prospects for the future, forces them to learn to live with shattered hopes and lessened expectations, and most of all directs their thinking inwards. As Emily Dickinson’s ailments had probably existed for a few years, she had mastered the art of introspection and self-examination which she later depicted in her verse – often as a metaphor. This way her poetry can be recognized as a personal myth and an extension of herself (2–5).

The majority of Dickinson’s poems were written in the early 1860s. It was during this time that the poet suffered from impaired vision and made two trips to Boston for treatment. During the rehabilitation she had to stay out of the light and have her eyes covered with a bandage. In a letter written in 1864 to her sister Lavinia she complained, “I have been sick so long I do not know the sun” (qtd. in Phillips 62). Her sickroom confinement gave rise to fears and suffering which found their expression in poem 327.

> Before I got my eye put out
> I liked as well to see –
> As other creatures, that have Eyes
> And know no other way – (Dickinson 155)

James Guthrie suggests two ways of interpreting this poem. The first assumes that the poet blames herself for losing her sight; she was disobedient and ignored the doctor's instructions to shun the light. The passion with which she admired the landscape must have overpowered her senses and she recklessly exposed her eyes to the sun at its zenith (15).

> The Meadows – mine –
> The Mountains – mine –
> All Forests – Stintless Stars –
> As much of Noon as I could take
> Between my finite eyes – (Dickinson 155)

Her hungry eyes devoured the light at noon, transgressing the limits of safety, which resulted in her blindness. The second interpretation is more metaphysical and relocates the blame to an external force. While absorbing and glorifying the beauty of nature, she perceived it to be as splendid as Paradise, thus revealing God's secret – that Earth resembles heaven. Her loss of sight was punishment for her premature view of God's abode. Towards the end of the poem she seems to accept her punishment and resorts to using the "soul" as a tool of perception. Yet the phrase "I got my eye put out" is not free from resentment. She does not understand why she had to be punished whereas other creatures can frivolously take pleasure in the magnificence of this world, oblivious to its dark side (Guthrie 16).

Vision impairment and convalescence became a theme in a few other poems. Poem 745 again mentions "The putting out of Eyes" (Dickinson 365). The speaker, this time, seems to be wiser and knows that there will be no improvement without sacrifice. The vision of the world has to be relinquished for a while if the "larger function" is to be achieved. "Renunciation – is a piercing Virtue – / The letting go" (365). But even though the speaker remembers to bandage her eyes the word "piercing" indicates how painful the process is. Preoccupation with her illness and lack of vision were also responsible for time disorientation as made evident in poem 425.

> Good Morning – Midnight –
> I'm coming Home –
> Day – got tired of Me –
> How could I – of Him? (Dickinson 203)

The narrator of the poem presents herself as a "little Girl" who was rejected by daylight and has to do with living in darkness. Her childishness is symbolic of the vulnerability and helplessness of a suffering person, "Sunshine was a sweet place" but morning did not like her so all she can do is to say "Goodnight – Day!" With all her cleverness the poet could not understand the injustice of having to live a nocturnal life (Guthrie 19).

Something was wrong with this world, or even the whole universe. This suspicion underlies poem 415.

> Sunset at Night – is natural –
> But Sunset on the Dawn
> Reverses Nature – Master –
> So Midnight's – due – at Noon (Dickinson 198)

"Sunset on the Dawn" indicates that stages of the day became indistinguishable. Day and night blend into one blackness. The beauty of midday and gratitude to God for its creation was replaced with a total darkness and cynical scepticism, expressed in words, "Jehovah's Watch – is wrong" (198). In poem 1018 Dickinson compares her state of a blind person to the sun, which like a sightless vagrant, blessed passers-by, without ever being blessed himself (Guthrie 20).

Even if in some letters there was a trace of hope detectable, the recuperation period was extremely difficult for the poet and her worst fear was that of not being able to read or write. In a letter to Joseph Lyman, in about 1865, Emily Dickinson wrote:

> Some years ago I had a woe, the only one that ever made me tremble. It was shutting out of all the dearest ones of time, the strongest friends of the soul-BOOKS [.] The medical man said avaunt ye tormentors, he also said 'down thoughts, & plunge into her soul.' He might have as well have said, 'Eyes be blind,' 'heart be still.' So I had eight months of Siberia (qtd. in Guthrie 10).

Luckily, the poet did not shut her books, and what is more, the painful experience provided her with inspiration for her artistic productivity and shaped her poetic voice. Even though reading a poem based on biographical evidence is often considered "reductive and simplistic" (Guthrie 5) not taking the personal experience into account may mean underestimating the intimacy between literary creation and the individual life of the poet (5).

Fred White shows in his book how Maryanne Grabowsky finds some of Dickinson's poems indicative of agoraphobia – another illness which troubled the poet. Grabowsky says:

> As we look through the fascicle poems, we recognise the pattern of agoraphobic life-style: the flight from fears, the need for protection within the father's house, the atmosphere of family conflict, and the desire for release from tormenting inner pressure (qtd. in White 61).

Symptoms of agoraphobia, as described by Grabowsky, can be found in poem 324. The first lines: "Some keep the Sabbath going to Church / I keep it, staying at home" (Dickinson 153) are interpreted as traces of the fear of crowds and public gatherings (White 61). However, considering Dickinson's lifelong rebellion against established religion and its tenets, these lines do not constitute strong evidence of agoraphobia. As another example of a poem that arose from the poet's fear Grabowsky mentions poem 410, "The first Day's Night had come – / And grateful that a thing / So terrible – had been endured – / I told my Soul to sing –" (Dickinson 195). She comments on this poem as follows:

> In this poem, Dickinson records her reaction to a complete, full blown panic attack, something that left 'her Strings snapt' and 'Her Bow – to Atoms blown.' ...What she is describing here are two major effects of a panic attack: the first is a fear of recurrence and the second is the fear of personality disintegration (qtd. in White 61).

Grabowsky finishes her book with the statement that Emily Dickinson used her words as a weapon to defend herself against the daunting world that overpowered her. Words had a magical power that helped the poet to liberate herself from the emotional torture that accompanied her so often (White 62).

John Cody proposes a psychoanalytic reading of Emily Dickinson's verse. Close analysis of poems and family letters leaves him with no doubt that the poet suffered from prostration and is surprised that anyone may miss such an interpretation. He asserts that no-one, not even a poet, is likely to depict emotional states that are foreign to them, especially with such accuracy and profundity as Emily Dickinson did. The writer warns that not taking the biographical element into account and not seeing the full intensity of the poet's suffering may result in misunderstanding and trivializing much of her work. He traces the development of Emily Dickinson's illness through her poems and distinguishes between poems which depict mild depressive moods and ones revealing disabling psychosis (291–295).

The onset of the illness is usually marked by a slight melancholy and despondency. According to Cody poem 111 bears traces of such moods (296). The cheerfulness that nature evokes is entwined with a gentle sadness: "Wherefore mine eye thy silver mists / Wherefore, Oh Summer's Day" (Dickinson 53). Another example is poem 353, which presents a futile attempt to stay happy despite the misery of life:

> A happy lip – breaks sudden –
> It doesn't state you how
> It contemplated – smiling –
> Just consummated – now – (Dickinson 167)

"A happy lip" considered smiling, but the smile was not a spontaneous reaction – rather a forced one, pretended, like the one in poem 514: "Her smile was shaped like other smiles – " (Dickinson 251). The speaker tries to conceal her internal sadness by projecting a happy appearance, but in vain. Her smile is compared to a lonely bird which somewhere above, with no listeners at all sings to forget its pain.

Thoughts about suicide appeared at the beginning of her ailment but their portrayal in verse is rather romantic and sentimental and the poet appears to play with the thought rather than consider it seriously. In poem 146 the poet speculates if anyone would miss her if she suddenly died "On such a night or such a night / Would anybody care / If such a little figure / Slipped quiet from its chair –" (Dickinson 69). Despite the seriousness of the theme the mood seems calm and light. The poems portraying the most devastating pain, arising from the centre of the darkest experience, were written between 1858 and 1862 (Sewall 501). Even if some biographers doubt that Emily Dickinson suffered from insanity, the fact remains that during this time her work depicts a mind which, under a heavy weight of despair, no longer obeys her. In the poem "The first Day's Night had come" her lyrical "I," which survived a psychotic episode, depicts her traumatic experience and fears of insanity.

> My Brain – began to laugh –
> I mumbled – like a fool –
> And tho''tis years ago – that Day –
> My Brain keeps giggling – still
>
> And Something's odd – within-
> That person that I was –
> And this One – do not feel the same -–
> Could it be Madness – this? (Dickinson 195)

The line "My Brain- began to laugh" illustrates division within the personality. The speaker's feelings and responses are no longer integrated: while one part of the ego reacts in a very unusual way, the second one watches the performance as if from a distance. The hysterical laughter is as disturbing as the loss of control over speech articulation in line 2 of the same stanza. The speaker tries to express herself coherently, but instead mumbles in an inefficient way. The final stanza reveals the speaker's awareness of the mental disjunction. She realizes that there is something strange in her present self and full of terror asks a rhetorical question "Could it be Madness – this?" (Cody 318).

Another poem which explores the brain function and presents its disintegration is poem 280 "I felt a funeral, in my Brain" (Dickinson 128). Through the allegory of a funeral ritual the poet tries to exteriorize what is happening inside the speaker's mind. The first few stanzas depict the successive stages of burial ceremony: the arrival of mourners, the church service, the lifting of the coffin and tolling of the bells. The progress of the sequential phases is, however, slowed down and disturbed by the repetitions of some actions: treading – treading / beating – beating – /... those same Boots of Lead, again, / ...Space– began to tall, / I dropped down, and down – / And hit a World, at every plunge." These repetitions of obsessive thinking disclose the speaker's descent into madness. She feels mounting irritation with everything that is going on around, but cannot do anything. The sounds and movements keep "beating" on her mind until it starts going "numb." The psychological torture continues until her final remark stops in mid-sentence with the word "then." As the unconscious cannot be satisfied with an acceptable conclusion, and the wounded soul feels that nothing more can happen in life, the poem finishes with an inconclusive utterance (Vendler *Poets thinking*, 73–74). The events are related in retrospect and they offer an explanation of what happened to the speaker in the past. The funeral she participated in produced such an overwhelming sense of loneliness and resignation that she suddenly felt as if it was her own burial and her own coffin. She feels so defeated that she does not even share her feelings with the reader but recounts the events in a matter of fact manner. The mourners are anonymous and faceless, no words are spoken, and the speaker is in complete mental isolation. The synecdoche in the line "And Being, but an Ear" reduces the people, whom she calls "some strange Race," to being only listeners. While her personal drama is going on, the mourners are performing a ritual "With those same Boots of Lead, again." This natural order of things and solemn character is emphasized by the classic ballad meter and rhythm, which is similar to a funeral hymn. The last stanza emphasizes that the speaker's suffering has no end. Even after she has died she isn't simply buried but she feels how she "dropped down, and down – / And hit a world at every plunge." Despite the physical pain implied by words "break" and "hit" the speaker feels the terror of falling into the abyss – the unknown. And again she is completely helpless and alone. Paula Bennet observed, "There is neither a sustaining God nor a sustaining scaffold of meaning to support her. Like the trapdoor on a gallows or like the planks supporting a coffin until it is dropped into the grave, the 'bottom' drops out of reality" (34). The dramatic ending, "And Finished knowing – then" states our ignorance about what is "beyond the grave" and leaves room for some speculation.

As maintained by John Cody, at the height of her instability and psychic disintegration Emily Dickinson must have experienced the most crushing anguish, so mighty that her thinking processes became chaotic and she could no longer link ideas or make logical connections. The enigmatic phrase, from one of her letters, of having a "snarl in the brain" (qtd. in Cody 393) becomes less obscure when we compare it with poem 937.

I felt a Cleaving in my Mind –
As if my Brain had split –

I tried to match it – Seam by Seam –
But could not make them fit. (Dickinson 439)

Just like in the poem "And then a Plank in Reason broke / And I dropped down" (Dickinson 128) the poet undergoes a split of consciousness and the link with reality is broken. The brave attempt to connect the splintered parts and to restore the previous state of mind sets the poem in motion only to finish, however, in total failure: "But Sequence ravelled out of Sound / Like Balls – upon a floor" (440). The image of balls rolling disorderly in all direction creates a sense of hopelessness; it is no longer possible to achieve a coherent sequence. The poet has no control over her mind anymore. The precision of thought and disciplined intellect indicate that this sort of poem must have been written in retrospect, but the profound insight into the specific kind of pain tends to endorse John Cody's hypothesis that the poet drew upon knowledge from her own experience (295).

With the development of her illness Emily Dickinson came to know the "real" pain, the one beyond endurance, which not only immobilises, but pushes one into self-destructive action. In a letter to Austin, when his marriage was crumbling, Emily observed "Sorrow is unsafe when it is real sorrow" (qtd. in Cody 298). Similar concern is expressed in a letter to Higginson after his wife's death: "I cannot resist to write again, to ask if you are safe? Danger is not at first, for then we are unconscious, but in the after – slower – Days" (qtd. in Cody 298). The poem "After great pain, a formal feeling comes" (Dickinson 162) describes the fragile emotional balance that a survivor of a recent trauma experiences. The poet illustrates with great precision the process of substituting feelings of agony with a conventional, superficial mode of behaviour. Even though the emotions seem to be as stable and firm as a gravestone, it is not strength that stabilizes them, but apathy. The "Heart" becomes "stiff," time is not important anymore, "Yesterday, or Centuries before," and memory does not seem to operate properly. While the first stanza concentrates on the inner changes, the second depicts automated, indifferent, directionless movements: "The Feet, mechanical, go around." The sense of numbed consciousness is enhanced by imagery characterized by possessing the qualities of lifelessness. The final lines of the poem compare this grief to death by freezing and the ultimate surrender.

Poem 686 shows how aware the poet was of the difference between hypothetical emotions and those experienced.

They say that 'Time assuages'–
Time never did assuage –
An actual suffering strengthens,
As Sinews do, with age – (Dickinson 339)

Probably written during the height of her emotional distress, this poem shows that truly intense pain does not accept any solace or hope for recuperation. The misery is so vast that even time cannot ease the pain. The poem states that the healing power of time is an illusion and that those who have been cured of sorrow never felt real pain. True pain stays with us. Even when the symptoms of despair disappear the harsh truth about life's brutality lingers and does not allow us to remain naïve and innocent. Pain is an eternal force, outside of time, as depicted in the poem "Pain – has an Element of Blank – / It cannot recollect / When it begun – or if there were / A time when it was not –" (Dickinson 650). Anguish renders time and history insignificant; nothing matters, nothing changes, just emptiness. The only thing that can ease pain is getting used to it. In the poem 252 the poet heroically asserts, "I can wade grief, / Whole pools of it – / I'm used to that" (Dickinson 115).

1.2. The Empowering side of suffering

Emily Dickinson's poems constitute a dialogue of numerous perspectives on the nature of pain. In the previous part of this chapter an attempt was made to present the insupportable dimension of suffering and trauma-related poetry. In this section the positive, life-enhancing aspect of pain, which helped the poet turn her anguish into vigour and greatness will be shown. The poems analysed in this section indicate the successful end of mourning and the poetic self-transcendence. All lacks are replaced with new compensatory aspects of life.

1.2.1. Suffering as a stimulus to greater self-understanding and creativity

> A work of art that insures the rebirth of its author and its reader or viewer is one that succeeds in integrating the artificial language it puts forward (new style, new composition, surprising imagination) and the unnamed agitations of an omnipotent self... such a fiction if it isn't an antidepressant, is at least a survival, a resurrection... (Kristeva 51)

In *An American Triptych* Wendy Martin observes that Emily Dickinson's emotional patterns reflect a Puritan doctrine which recognises suffering and self-renunciation as a sign of moral strength and even a victory. Paradoxically turmoil can lead to spiritual tranquillity. While investigating Emily Dickinson's poems we can discern the poet's transition from Puritanism to Romanticism in which an abiding, omnipotent God was replaced by a disobedient, guilt-ridden Byronic outlook. Only after rejecting the dichotomies of Calvinism was Emily Dickinson able to overcome her submissiveness and achieve maturity by facing the conflicts and contradictions of her life. The probable culmination of this metamorphosis was seeing herself as an "Empress of Calvary" (qtd. in Martin 102) who holds sway over her suffering. She became stronger not by denying her pain or suppressing it but by living through it and collecting some benefits out of it (102). She chose withdrawal as her lifestyle because such hardship stimulated compensatory fantasies and fed her art. While examining Emily Dickinson's poems we can trace this transformation process.

The first stage, undoubtedly, was the realization that pain is not without purpose; that it leads to a better appreciation of things and sharpens perception. Absence and nothingness, ironically, can be empowering because positive things gain value only when contrasted with negative ones. This truth became the theme of a multitude of poems. Poem 677 tells us that only in the light of the inscrutable reality of death, is one able to glorify life: "To be alive – is Power –" (Dickinson 335). Only through reevaluating our perspective can we experience ourselves as human beings and appreciate life's uniqueness remembering that it exists only once as stated in poem 1741 "That it will never come again / Is what makes life so sweet" (706). The poet revisits this motif repeatedly in her work. In "Success is counted sweet" (35) only those who know the value of success and nectar, feel the "sorest need" for it and the "definition so clear of Victory" is comprehensible only to the "defeated and dying." In poem 167 the lines "To learn the Transport by the Pain – / As Blind Men learn the sun!" (79) support the same viewpoint. Paradoxically, delight is only felt through lack and deprivation. Correspondingly, in poem 73, those "Who never lost, are unprepared / A Coronet to find" (38). These poems are textual evidence of Dickinson's keen awareness of the complicated truths of human desire. Whilst her isolation would suggest a poorer grasp of the gifts of life, she learned to appreciate them even more from a distance, by yearning for them. In other poems, such as "If your nerve deny you" (136) and "No rack can torture me –" (183) the poet celebrates the power of the self to rise itself above suffering and increase control over one's mind.

Having realized the power of her own intellect, the poet demands "Me, change! Me, alter!" (122). The small Daisy or the wounded bird from the "Master" letters searches for an autonomous and self-assured side; one that is not frightened of death or suffering, that can tolerate loss and is not tempted by the world's lures or God's promises. This little girl who "was the slightest in the House" and who "took the smallest Room" as expressed in poem 486 (234) soon recognizes her own potential as a poet and pursues a truly splendid goal – immortality. It was writing which was to ensure her deathlessness. Emily Dickinson did not seek fame "Fame is a fickle food / Upon a shifting plate" (677) or "one that does not stay" (623). She wanted to create an art which is a form of truth, an "amazing sense" distilled "From ordinary Meanings" (215). Only such art had a chance to survive in the "Ceaseless Rosemary" (335). Immortality became Emily Dickinson's fascination. This motif underlies much of her work. Among others, poem 406 presents eternity as precious as gold "Slow Gold – but Everlasting" (193) and poem 726, where she asks "Is that Great Water in the Wes t– / Termed Immortality –" (356). Poem 827 curtly informs that all the news the poet knows is "bulletins all day / From Immortality" (401). The poet likes musing about great art and timelessness but she also realizes that it is only achievable through self-denial and commitment.

In poem 675 writing poetry is compared to the brutal process of extracting perfume from roses.

> Essentials Oils – are wrung –
> The Attar from the Rose
> Be not expressed by Suns – alone –
> It is the gift of Screws – (Dickinson 335)

Both practices are painful and require some loss. Just as the rose petals must be crushed to obtain essence, the poet's life must be sacrificed to produce the "Attar" of her life – the poetry. But although transforming experience into lyrics involves "Screws", "wringing" and finally the death of the author as a woman, the reward is worth such suffering. The poet's work will stay alive even if confined to the limits of her "Drawer." Dickinson creates her self-portrait as a female poet striving towards immortality by using linguistic and metaphorical screws (Miller 3).

1.2.2. Adopting an unorthodox feminine role

> Disenchantment transformed into beauty is particularly perceptible in feminine portraits (Kristeva 127).

Knowing how to extract the positive aspect from deprivation, Emily Dickinson substituted longing for romantic love with an astute reflection on women's life and their secondary position in a patriarchal society. Already as a young girl she noticed the inequality between the genders. In a letter written, when she was twenty one, she described the relationship between wives and their husbands. Wives are depicted there like "sweet flowers at noon with their heads bowed in anguish before the mighty sun... which scorches them, scathes them; they have got through with peace" (qtd. in Cody 120). The "sun" which symbolizes the husband, is a domineering male who cruelly oppresses a "forgotten wife" (120). It is very possible that such an image of marriage was fostered by the situation in her own home. For Edward Dickinson women were inferior beings. He shared the nineteenth-century masculine belief that they were incapable of serious thought or ambition. Emily must have noticed the discrepancies in power and freedom between her parents and it must have affected her a great deal as a woman (120). But, unlike her submissive mother, she decided to express her resentment. In a letter to her friend Abiah Root, written in 1850, she complains:

> Father and Austin still clamor for food, and I, like a martyr am feeding them. Wouldn't you love to see me in these bonds of great despair, looking around my kitchen, and praying for such deliverance... *My* kitchen I think I call it, God forbid that it was, or shall be my own – God keep me from what they call *household*, except that bright one of "faith"! (qtd. in Martin, *The Cambridge Introduction to Emily Dickinson* 52).

What Emily Dickinson could not voice in public she included in her letters and poems. Even though she adored her father, her brother Austin, and some chosen men whose friendship she sought, Emily defied the stifling social conditions of her time. The letter cited above may have been a consequence of mounting resentment, or perhaps she already had in mind her creative future. Either way, she was beginning to oppose the basic expectations of women to forfeit their own lives and submit to their husbands. Rebellious by nature, Emily was unwilling to surrender to such a subservient position. Giving up one's independence was too high a price for her to pay for a marriage (Martin, *The Cambridge Introduction to Emily Dickinson* 52–76).

Believing it would be more acceptable to the public, Dickinson chose to disguise her condemnation in a deceptive conformity or irony. In poem 732 she does not critique the institution of marriage overtly, but uses a skilful interplay of form, syntax and sound.

> She rose to His Requirement – dropt
> The Playthings of Her Life
> To take the honorable Work
> Of Woman and of Wife – (Dickinson 359)

The seeming conformity to the orthodox female role is illustrated by the application of the ballad measure. The traditional meter and marriage, however, collide with irregular syntax. Just as a woman's happiness is upset by the limitations and burdens matrimony imposes on her, the regularity of the common meter is disrupted by the additional syllable "dropt." This word carries a pejorative semantic load as it indicates the end of a playful attitude to life and the loss of freedom that occurs with the commencement of marriage. The dash before the word creates a dramatic effect and forces the reader to stop and focus on its significance. Another potential disturbance to marital bliss is hinted at the development of "Pearl" and "Weed," which stand for subversive hidden energy. Both are the products of abnormal growth. Precious and luxurious, pearls are a status symbol and Emily Dickinson often employed them as a metaphor for poetry and feminine writing, whereas weeds are undesired and destructive plants. In this way marriage generates the "honorable work" but also, like a weed, chokes growth and autonomy. By packing the poem with alliteration and repetitions, the poet supplements the verse with another stratum of non-discursive connotation. The heavy "r" sound in the first line introduces some harshness in the poem and the alliterated "Work," "Woman," "Wife" and "Weed" represent all the associations that the poet makes with the married state. Emily Dickinson's iconoclastic attitude toward marriage aligns with her unorthodox use of grammar: strange use of the preposition "of" in "of Amplitude," irregular verb forms such as "dropt," and "be known" and the pronoun "Himself." The poem clearly states that the bliss of marriage is superficial and the "honorable Work" actually constitutes an act of submission and capitulation to the husband's overbearing supremacy (Sielke 38–39).

Another poem which echoes the previous discussion of language and semantic content is: "I rose – because He sank." This poem is a real manifestation of female self-empowerment. The hymn meter the poet applied here is a special measure to ensure protection and camouflage subversive visions.

> I rose – because He sank –
> I thought it would be opposite –
> But when his power dropped –
> My Soul grew straight (Dickinson 303)

Sielke reads this poem as not only the speaker's seizure of male strength but also male subjectivity. When she says "My Soul grew straight" and in the last line "I lifted Him" she does not do it with female frailty but by means of the supposed, Freudian, "phallic force" (Sielke 41) of hymn poetry, the "Thews of Hymn." The diminished male potency ("his power dropped"), apart from being displayed on a semantic level, is also visible in a "castrated" (41), conventional meter that lacks a regular rhyme scheme. The rhyming words that irregularly appear in the poem – "sinew," "knew," "grew" and "drew" – emphasize disorder and the growing female power ("thews") as well as unconscious knowledge ("ways I knew not that

I knew") associated with masculine potency via puns and inner rhymes such as "Hymn," "him" and "firm." Almost halfway through the poem the female – male "power play" is abandoned for a moment and the third stanza introduces a notion of gender equality and unity with "I met him – / Balm to Balm." This suggested union is enhanced by fitting versification. Although the sentence is cut in half the distance from "I" to "him" is very small and the identification between subject and object is aided by parallelism and end-rhyme. Soon, however, we find that this evenness of gender power is not possible here on earth but only beyond the "Grave," when the body ("low Arch of Flesh") is eliminated. Camille Paglia suggests that by rejecting her passive female identity Dickinson makes "transsexual leaps into eternity" (qtd. in Sielke 41). She projects fantasies of completion into infinities. The rise of female dominance and the shift in sexual hierarchy is accentuated by the radical contrast of line lengths in the last stanza: a ten-syllable line is followed by a four-syllable one: "And ways I knew not that I knew – till then – / I lifted Him –" The last line is a display of unmediated female supremacy. Interestingly, when Todd and Higginson suggested publishing the poem Arlo Bates cut the last two stanzas, perhaps believing that the gender equality would be a better received conclusion of the poem than the female superiority manifested by the last words. However, the poem was only published in 1929 with stanzas 2 and 3 removed (42).

One of the most powerful poems, which takes an ironic look at the marriage state, is poem 1072 "Title divine – is mine!"

> The title divine – is mine!
> The Wife – without the Sign!
> Acute Degree - conferred on me –
> Empress of Calvary!
> (...)
> Born – Bridalled – Shrouded –
> In a Day – (Dickinson 487)

The poet describes love, which in its disappointment equals the Calvary experience. Just like Jesus, through his crucifixion, the speaker became a messiah; the poem's speaker through her mortifying marriage becomes the "Empress of Calvary." In the expression "Acute Degree" Martha Smith discerns the acronym A.D. and interprets it not as "the year of our Lord" (37) but a time of the speaker's grief. The line "Born – Bridalled – Shrouded –" juxtaposes life and death with the "Bridalled" in between. In one day the newly wedded woman is born and dressed for death. Bridalled refers to a wedding but it can also be read as "bridled" which would mean controlled and restrained. The marital images mingle with those of death and subordination (37). Speaking with an independent voice, the fulfilled poet uses biblical symbolism to "challenge the social, sexual, and religious ideologies that eclipse and shroud women's lives" (Pollack 157). A different interpretation is proposed by Beth Doriani who suggests that the speaker assumes a status of the betrothed to the Emperor of Calvary. She condemns marriage in the temporal world and depicts her own divine, royal matrimony to the king not in terms of dutiful servitude but as an elevation in status (86). Whatever version we accept it is undeniable that Emily Dickinson rejects the possibility of earthly marriage as it suppresses the "Royal" (Dickinson 487) self and she chooses to be faithful to her vocation. This poem was written, according to Johnson's dating, at about the same time as the "Master" letters and represents the emergence of a sovereign and assertive poet from the struggle with fragility and smallness (Martin, *The Cambridge introduction to Emily Dickinson* 83).

Dickinson's deep desire for love and friendship often made her dependent on others, which was in conflict with her aspiration for autonomy. However, she overcomes her "smallness" and manages to transform her emotional suffering into artistic productivity, which in turn gives her liberty and power. "Dickinson no longer belongs to others; she is her own 'Master' and she will relinquish herself to no one" (Martin, *The Cambridge Introduction to Emily Dickinson* 85). This attitude permeates another poem, "I'm ceded – I've stopped being theirs" (Dickinson 247), which supposedly comes from this same period. The dependent Emily, who as a child belonged to her society and was obedient to the wishes of her parents, is gone, and so are her dolls. She inherited the old existence and could not decide anything. Now she can make her own decisions and determine her own future. She is no longer the "half unconscious Queen" (247). Full of determination she opts for the "Crown" and chooses her "second Rank" (247). Not needing anyone to christen her, she baptizes herself unto a new mission, a poetic vocation. The crown symbolizes not only royalty but also a laurel wreath presented to poets (Martin, *The Cambridge Introduction to Emily Dickinson* 85).

There were other nineteenth century women writers complaining about domestic restraints, however not many managed to evade them as successfully as Emily Dickinson. Despite some evidence of her passionate love for the "Master" and a relationship with Judge Otis P. Lord, which resulted in his marriage proposal, matrimony and motherhood did not attract the poet. Judging by standards of ordinary people, for whom fulfilment means family, children and a successful career, Emily Dickinson's life, may seem very dull and unrewarded. But the poet was by no means average. She was exceptionally talented and intelligent and did not allow anyone or anything to limit her freedom. She also elevated herself above the mundane home duties of everyday life. "I don't keep the moth part of the House – I keep the Butterfly part" (qtd. in Bennett 12) she admitted in one of her letters, and this was confirmed by her sister who declared "Emily was a very busy person herself. She had to think – she was the only one of us who had that to do" (12). Emily Dickinson did her share of household chores but the "poetess" persona she became was much closer to her heart. She turned into a woman of very strong convictions and was not afraid to voice them.

1.2.3. Poetry as a sublimation of rage

> My necessary Thing is also and absolutely my enemy, my foil, the delightful focus of my hatred (Kristeva 15).

Emily Dickinson, who was perceived as a gentle and a shy woman concealed a lot of anger under her calm exterior. Several factors contributed to the fact that the poet felt cheated by fate. Feeling unhappy about her looks, which she expressed in one of her letters: "Myself the only Kangaroo among the Beauty" (Cody 439), disappointed by God, deserted by some of her friends, unloved by her mother, Emily Dickinson hid a lot of aggression that eventually found an outlet in her verse. The poet had a strong, masculine streak in her which derived from identification with her dominant father. John Cody traces it back to the oedipal stage when Emily turned to her father as a source of sensual love and unconsciously adopted his masculine perspective of life. She resented being a weak woman like her mother and cherished her powerful and defiant spirit. Anger became a constructive factor and her defence mechanism against harmful, self-debasing emotions that often overwhelmed her.

One of the symbols representing the depth of emotions and repressed expression is the volcano, which although outwardly serene seethes with turbulent inner life. Volcanoes represent an unpredictable, subversive force, which is extremely violent when released because of the energy accumulated during its dormant years. They also convey an image of devastating linguistic utterance erupting out of silence.

> A still – Volcano – Life –
> That flickered in the night –
> When it was dark enough to do
> Without erasing sight –
> A quiet – Earthquake Style –
> Too subtle to suspect (Dickinson 295)

These lines of the poem, which are highly compressed and self-reflective, are "an enactment of the thematic and stylistic polarities of American women's literature" (Martin, *The Cambridge introduction to Emily Dickin-*

son 183). The oxymoronic "Still – Volcano – Life –" and "A quiet – Earthquake Style –" emphasize the misleading calmness that often camouflages real passion or "explosiveness beneath a mild demeanor" (Petrino 196). The speaker, positioned near Naples, alludes to Pompeii – the city once destroyed by a volcano. In the line "The Solemn – Torrid – Symbol –" the word "symbol" clearly states that the volcano stands for something else, perhaps the suffering, which although articulated, was never correctly comprehended by the people that surrounded the poet. "The lips that never lie" know the risk of expressing secret thoughts honestly. Truth-telling is potentially destructive, especially when the lips were to erupt with a repressed, discontented feminine voice. The compression of two lines hint at the merciless power: "Whose hissing Corals part – and shut – / And Cities – ooze away –" (Dickinson 295) The ominous silence detectable throughout the poem is disrupted by the sound of "hissing Corals." Just as the volcano that erupts from within its constraints of rock, the poet's language bursts limitations imposed by social rules and language conventions. The chaos brought about by this explosion is intensified by compression, elision, ubiquitous dashes and a shattered structure. This irregular prosody reflects fervent emotions brought under restraint. One such irregularity is Dickinson's use of adjectives, which does not follow normal grammatical rules. For instance, instead of "volcanic" she prefers a noun "volcano." Her lines are difficult to understand as they lack a clearly defined grammatical subject. Infinitives "to do" and "to suspect" unattached to any subject generate a sense of universality but also render the sentences incoherent. Also the use of enjambment between stanzas hinders the understanding of meaning. It is impossible to understand the second stanza without reading the last line of the first one (Petrino 196–198). The departure from conventional discourse, however, only enriches the poet's verse and makes it open to multiple interpretations.

Poem number 1146 is another which presents the power of speech through the image of a volcano.

> When Etna basks and purrs
> Naples is more afraid
> Then when she shows her Garnet Tooth –
> Security is loud – (Dickinson 513)

The words "bask and purr" immediately bring to mind the image of a sleeping cat. It is not, however, a serene image: "Naples is more afraid." This peace and silence is suspicious and ominous. Volcanoes, like cats, are unpredictable. The crucial effect of the poem is achieved by the final word, which paradoxically states that a loud voice creates a sense of security. It is better when the volcano rumbles and roars because then we know what to expect, and so we feel more secure. As we always associate noise with calamities, the poet defamiliarises this concept and the reader has a chance to look at it in a new way. Thus "the deviation from the conceptual norm may function as a device to re-conceptualise the world" (van Peer 201). By drawing an analogy to speech, we may infer that the ability to voice her opinions loudly may give a woman a sense of security. Keeping emotions suppressed and silenced can lead to a destructive explosion, as even the gentlest cat has a "Garnet Tooth."

In poem 1677 a volcano is the poet's meditative spot, dormant for so long that it became covered by grass: "On my volcano grows the Grass / A meditative spot –" Looking calm and peaceful it seems the right place for birds to nestle. But the poet warns later:

> How red the Fire rocks below
> How insecure the sod
> Did I disclose
> Would populate with awe my solitude (Dickinson 685).

The placid exterior hides a volatile interior. The image of volcano again exemplifies the duality of the female writer's nature, which often, despite a benign appearance, is raging inside with rebellious visions. The defiance of conformity is also displayed by means of structure. A woman's repressed speech can unfold in the same way as a tetrameter expands into pentameter rhythm in the last line. Not having to shape her work to the public taste Dickinson presents a very open and sincere view on woman's self-sacrifice and renunciation. Her poems reveal "feeling of solidarity" with underprivileged women (Petrino 199).

In the poem "My life had stood as – a Loaded Gun" Dickinson fuses fantasies of power with realities of repression and helplessness. Adrienne Rich looks upon this poem as a form of aggression and a show of subversive power. Experiencing herself as a loaded gun, Emily Dickinson was aware of the deadly potential of the arsenal of words that women poets possess. She also claims that this poem is a central work for understanding Dickinson and the circumstances in which the poet lived. Rich envisages Dickinson confined to her father's house, harbouring a rage and rebellious thoughts which had probably accumulated for years. Emily Dickinson objected to being perceived as a recluse who was responsible for cooking, housekeeping and gardening. Even when doing her household tasks, she regarded herself as an artist, often writing her poems on torn envelopes or the back of a grocery list (Grabher, Hagenbüchle, Miller 344). Any sort of underrating on the part of others found an outlet in her work. In the poem "My life had stood as – a Loaded Gun" the speaker seeks empowerment through her unification with the "Owner" who carries her away and through their love they become one. Together they merge into one royal, powerful "We," which enables the speaker to exercise her hunting or other faculties. She presents herself as a daring feminist and a mighty aggressor, who is very protective of her master. She not only does all the hunting for him but also guards him from danger. But in all her fusion of love and death with him, she is still dependent on him; she must be "carried" by him. The poem, thus, is an illustration of "the limitations experienced by woman under patriarchy" or a female artist who needs a protector to support her in her career (Farr 244). The "Vesuvian face" implies the anger of a repressed woman as she realizes that the invented power is an illusion (Martin, *The Cambridge Introduction to Emily Dickinson* 187). For Sandra Gilbert and Susan Gubar the enraged and assertive Dickinson represents the split in the nineteenth century woman writer between "her conventional role in society and her creativity, between the Angel in the House and the madwoman in the attic" (qtd. in Grabher, Hagenbüchle, Miller 344).

A real display of strong emotions is manifested in poem 528.

> Mine – by the Right of the White Election!
> Mine – by the Royal Seal!
> Mine – by the Sign in the Scarlet prison –
> Bars-cannot conceal! (Dickinson 258)

It is one of Dickinson most exclamatory and emphatic works. It can be read as a wild affirmation of self which is assertive and demanding. Her rage is still detectable, but the tone alters from frustrated anger to confident, lawful independence. The poem is packed with vocabulary drawn from the legal profession: the words "Seal," "Repeal," Titled," "Charter" and "Steal" call attention to the idea of ownership and are strongly linked to the issues of autonomy and status. The whole poem leaves no place for doubt; the speaker with authoritative posturing claims her rights while expressing a sort of urgency and desperation. What adds to the tone of self-assertion, which is almost "Delirious," is a pattern of rhymes. The same end rhyme appears in both stanzas (Seal / conceal / Repeal / steal) and there are two internal rhymes (Right / White / Mine / Sign). The rhyme words contain high – front vowels "i" and "e," which together with some alliterations create an effect of "noisy excess. Undoubtedly, however, the most distinctive feature of the poem is the obsessive use of the possessive pronoun "Mine." The capitalized and separated with dashes "Mine" as well as the exclamation marks give the poem force and a sense of wild confident exultation (Small 129).

Emily Dickinson has learned how to use anger as a source of energy. In his book *An American Triptych* Martin repeats Adrienne Rich's words "I think anger can be a kind of genius if it's acted on" (197). Anger can liberate one from unacceptable social forms, as well as sustain during solitude. "The dialectic of rebellion is based on the conversion of despair into anger, dissatisfaction into action" (Kameen 89). In contrast to depression which acts in a paralysing way, rage can empower and be used constructively (89). Emily Dickinson's poetry constitutes evidence of this phenomenon.

1.2.4. New spirituality

> There is nothing more dismal than a dead God... (Kristeva 8)

Even though Emily Dickinson wrestled with God all her life she could not live without Him. A world without everything that God embodies – love, forgiveness, hope, beauty – would have been an empty world. Unable to accept the conventional Puritanism she kept seeking meaning and God elsewhere. The movement that influenced her most was Transcendentalism. Its main tenets held that one could transcend the mortal world through contemplation, intuition and a direct relationship with nature. Emily Dickinson was not a Transcendentalist; however she read books by Emerson, who visited Austin and Sue twice in 1857 and 1865. Her philosophy reflected the truths he advocated. She regarded nature as a source of knowledge, transferred her adoration from God to people and rejected church as an intermediary between people and the Almighty. In one of her letters she wrote: "Mr S. Preached in our church last Sabbath upon 'predestination,' but I do not respect 'doctrines,' and did not listen to him" (Martin, *The Cambridge Introduction to Emily Dickinson* 54). She found her own individual way for metaphysical experiences of which love and compassion were the main virtues.

This new spirituality shaped not only her style of life but also her writing. The most distinctive text in which she refuses to attend church is poem 324.

> Some keep the Sabbath going to Church –
> I keep it, staying at Home –
> With a Bobolink for a Chorister –
> And an Orchard, for a Dome – (Dickinson 153)

The opening line emphasises the preference for personal contact with God, away from crowds and religious dogmas. She would rather listen to a songbird than a leader of a choir. This verse testifies to the fact that she looks for God in silence and contemplation of nature. The next stanza supports this view. The orchard is where the wonders of this world are best observed. In the lines: "Some keep the Sabbath in Surplice – / I just wear my Wings –" (153) she may be saying that while others wear ostentatious gowns and demonstrate their faith, she wears wings – her modesty – which raises her up to God. True spirituality is not achieved by pretentious piety, but by finding peace within oneself. Only then do the riches of the church (the Dome) and its rituals stop being important. The poet juxtaposes "an Orchard" with "a Dome" to praise simplicity and nature as opposed to the materialistic and corrupted world of possession. Although others ensure heaven for themselves by attending church services, she does not because home is her paradise: "So instead of getting to Heaven, at last – / I'm going, all along" (154). These last two lines specify that through a spiritual unity with God one can feel His presence even at home, so she does not need a special place of worship to meet God – home is her private church. Heaven, too, stops being her destination, since she wants to concentrate on life on earth and people, rather than God alone.

Love of nature became a type of faith for Emily Dickinson. She believed in its power to elevate spiritually. Fascinated with the treasures of this world the poet studied and described the natural world in its minutest detail. This intimate relationship with the universe pulled her, however, further from the biblical God. She wrote to Susan:

> But the world allured me &... I listened to her syren voice... Friends reasoned with me & told me of the danger I was in... but I had rambled too far to return & ever since my heart has been growing harder & more distant (Martin, *The Cambridge Introduction to Emily Dickinson* 66).

She realised that the conformist way of life would have been easier and safer but also knew that church ceremonies and their Scriptural basis did not agree with her intuition. Poem 476 perfectly illustrates the change that happened in the poet's attitude toward her old religion: "I grown shrewder – scan the Skies / With a suspicious Air –" (Dickinson 230). With disillusionment about heaven came a strong sentiment for her garden and the natural surroundings.

She identified with nature and worshiped it. In poem 130 summer is presented as a "Sacrament" and "Last Communion" (Dickinson 61) and in poem 1408 she compares earth to paradise: "Earth is Heaven – / Whether Heaven is Heaven or not" (602). The real "Heaven," as stated in poem 239, is "The Apple on the Tree –" and "The Color, on the Cruising Cloud –" In some poems nature becomes her new religion and all the creatures it's congregation. Poem 1591 paints an image of "The Presbyterian Birds" (659) that are ready to "resume the Meeting" (659) and start praying. The most surprising is, however, poem 18 which depicts the death of summer. The first four line stanza informs that the gentian's petals are decaying and Maple leaves are red. The death of the season is followed by a funeral service and a procession.

It was a short procession,
The Bobolink was there –
An aged Bee addressed us –
And then we knelt in prayer –
We trust that she was willing –
We ask that we may be.
Summer – Sister – Seraph!
Let us go with thee!

In the name of the Bee –
And of the Butterfly –
And of the Breeze – Amen! (Dickinson 14)

The members of the procession are the Bobolink bird, an old Bee and a Butterfly. After the sermon was delivered by the Bee they prayed. The line "We trust that she was willing" Leiter interprets as willingness to die. She compares it to Dickinson's letter written to the minister Benjamin Newton asking if "he was willing to die" (26). Having understood that the summer is accepting God's will by departing for heaven the mourners pray that one day they do the same. The peaceful mood of approval is, however, broken by a sudden change in rhythm. The line "Summer – Sister – Seraph!" which introduces the emphatic trochaic meter into an iambic poem sounds like a cry of longing. The poet calls summer her sister and Seraph – an angel – which indicates a strong emotional bond and a wish for reunion. The three entities create the first trinity in this poem. The second one is formed by the Bee, the Butterfly and the Breeze. By establishing this new divine union Dickinson declares "an alternate spiritual universe" (27). Disappointed with the cruelty and injustice of the biblical God, the poet found her peace in the harmony of nature. Through identification with its creatures and plants she felt a part of the natural world. It became her means to achieve mortal transcendence.

Another subject of her adoration became her friends. Friendship occupied one of the central places in her faith and prayers. The strongest love she ever felt was for her sister-in-law, Sue. In one of the letters to her she describes her thoughts during pastor's prayers:

> (...) when he said "Our Heavenly Father," I said "Oh Darling Sue"; when he read the 100th Psalm, I kept saying your precious letter all over to myself, and Susie, when they sang... I made up words and kept singing how I loved you, and you had gone, while the rest of the choir were singing Hallelujahs (qtd. in Martin, *The Cambridge Introduction to Emily Dickinson* 64).

The attention that she was supposed to pay to God was reallocated to her friends. She treated friendship very earnestly and often referred to it using biblical language. In poem 203 the poet regards forgetting a friend a serious offence and compares it to Peter's denial of Christ (Martin, *The Cambridge Introduction to Emily Dickinson* 65).

> He forgot – and I – remembered –
> 'Twas an everyday affair –
> Long ago as Christ and Peter –
> "Warmed them" at the "Temple fire" (Dickinson 95).

By lifting companionship to the level of religious experience the poet makes a point that a friend should never be denied or rejected (Martin 65). The poet believed that a true friendship, just like the love of nature, was a way to achieve sublime spirituality.

Transcendentalists also believed that people could obtain salvation through hard work, individualism and self-reliance. All these ideas influenced Emily Dickinson as a person and a poet. Individualism was most visible in her life-style and the manner of writing. Unconventional grammar, unorthodox meter and syntax are the results of her instincts and a non-conformist approach to life. She often praised good work in her poems and elevated everyday domestic tasks to the spiritual level. Poem 219 depicts an ordinary act of cleaning.

> She sweeps with many-coloured Brooms –
> And leaves the Shreds behind –
> Oh Housewife in the Evening West –
> Come back, and dust the Pond! (Dickinson 101)

Martin observes that the poem presents "a powerful woman who transcends mere housework and 'leaves the Shreds behind' while ambitiously heading unfettered straight for the skies" (57). The magic power is demonstrated by aligning the activity of sweeping with the progression of the sunset, which suggests that the housewife has power over the heavens (57).

Dickinson not only believed in hard work and self-reliance but also practised it in her life. She made work – literary production – the objective of her life. As a poet she often identified herself with a bee, which was one of her symbols of diligence. Morgan notices that Dickinson "uses the image to convey poetic vocation as a form of industry which acquires spiritual significance within her poems (the poet 'gathers' as the bee, as full an experience of life as possible and 'stores' it within the poem)" (179). Poem 1755 presents a metaphor of the poetic work.

> To make a prairie it takes a clover and one bee,
> One clover, and a bee,
> And revery.
> The revery alone will do,
> If bees are few (Dickinson 710)

The poet, in an optimistic tone, asserts that it does not need that much to accomplish something meaningful. The major components are “a clover” (the material), “a bee” (the poet, or the worker) and “revery” (the dream). The poem appears to allude to the American Dream and sounds like an encouragement for creativity or poetic advice. The line “The revery alone will do” stresses the importance of having aspirations and the boldness to pursue one’s dream. Transcendentalism helped Emily Dickinson to develop her own private religion which became her lifestyle – away from the crowd and pretentiousness, but true to herself, nature and her friends.

1.3. Conclusion: Emotional disturbance as a prerequisite of a poetic explosion

Chapter One presented a biographical lack and its conquering in the poetic texts. The analysed poems show how the dynamic poetic process was closely linked to Emily Dickinson’s life experiences. The amount of poetry written in the years of her greatest suffering is evidence that emotional disturbance is a prior condition for the poet’s creativity. Mamunes presents some statistics concerning this occurrence. He notes that the year 1866 was a turning point in Emily Dickinson’s literary output. Her poetic drive dropped dramatically, from more than 200 poems written in the year 1865 to 70 written in the next five years combined. According to Alfred Habegger this decrease was due to the changes in the emotional life of the poet: “Beginning in 1858, the poet’s heroic production had been driven in part by the working-out of inner matters” (qtd. in Mamunes 151) but after 1865 Dickinson had achieve “a relaxed sense of security, a mature and detached perspective of herself” (151). George Mamunes recognizes in this the sense of security attained in the fifth and final stage of the grieving process. After denial, anger, bargaining, and depression the poet seemed to have achieved acceptance. As her health stabilized, and there were no more deaths around her, her emotions became soothed and so was the torrent of her artistic outpouring. “No longer a wounded deer, or a smitten rock that gushes, she averaged only 15 new poems a year from 1866 to 1870” (151). Paraphrasing the poet “We outgrow love, like other things” (Dickinson 420) one could say that we outgrow pain like other things, “put it in the Drawer” (420) and never come back to it again.

Chapter 2

Kristeva's Main Tenets

Chapter Two is devoted to the presentation of suffering as an integral part of Emily Dickinson's linguistic style and her poetic strategies. It introduces the major concepts of Julia Kristeva's theory; that is the notion of abjection, the semiotic and the symbolic and presents their reflection in Emily Dickinson's verse.

2.1. Kristeva's concept of abjection and Emily Dickinson's poetry

Julia Kristeva, a Bulgarian-French feminist, semiotician and a professor at the University of Paris is also a leading figure in international critical analysis and cultural studies. She was one of the people who helped to formulate post-structuralism. Her central focus became the speaking being and the signifying processes through which it is established. She was not happy with structuralist theory, which concentrated on meaning without paying enough attention to the speaking subject. She remarked: "Structural linguistics and the ensuing structural movement seem to explore epistemological space by eliminating the speaking subject" (Niall 72). For Kristeva the speaking being is in a constant state of change and exposed to different forces: inner drives, sexuality, cultural norms (McAfee 1). She rejects the idea of a subject detached from the world and its body. By applying psychoanalytic studies she presents evolution of the self and its relation to the evolution of language.

Black Sun is a moving contemplation on depression and melancholia. However, Kristeva is not interested in it as an illness but as a discourse with a special language that should be analysed. Drawing on Freud's description of melancholia and depression, Kristeva tries to examine the main issues connected with *object loss*, which is the maternal body. She maintains that language starts with a *negation of loss* (43). A "normal" person regains the lost object in speech: "'I have lost an essential object that happens to be, in final analysis, my mother,' is what the speaking being seems to be saying. 'But no, I have found her again in signs or rather since I consent to lose her I have not lost her (that is the negation), I can recover her in language'" (43). Thus, instead of suppressing sadness the person expresses it. This way the lost thing is not gone but survives in language and mourning is completed. Imagination and sublimation become an outcome of grieving. Kristeva states that "If I did not agree to lose mother, I could neither imagine nor name her" (41). Imagination – the ability of representation – starts with the acceptance of loss and it is only through this deficiency that desire and creativity are born.

The analysis of Emily Dickinson's texts reveals that, to a great extent, the poet's verse parallels Julia Kristeva's theory of mourning for the lost Thing. Poem 546 sounds like a manifestation of this theory.

> To fill a Gap
> Insert the Thing that caused it –
> Block it up Other –
> and 'twill yawn the more –
> You cannot solder an Abyss
> With Air (Dickinson 266)

This short poem suggests that the only way to deal with a loss is to keep it alive by writing about it. That is also the only method to deal with melancholia – to overcome it through language. Dickinson reveals profound self-knowledge in her verse.

For the depressive subject the maternal object becomes not "an Object" but a "lost Thing" that cannot be recaptured, something enticing and elusive. It is a memory of identity with the mother before separation. Kristeva defines it as "the real that does not lend itself to signification, the centre of attraction and repulsion, seat of sexuality from which the object of desire will become separated" (13). While a healthy person becomes reconciled with the loss through identification with "father in individual prehistory" (13), which is the symbolic order, the depressive subject is riveted to the maternal body. For the melancholy person the Thing is the endless void that cannot be compensated and with which the mourning person cannot part. Kristeva writes: "My depression points to my not knowing how to lose" (5).

The relationship of the depressed subject towards the lost thing oscillates between love and hate "I love that object, but even more so I hate it... and in order not to lose it I imbed it in myself" (Kristeva 11). This incorporation, however, disrupts the ego and breaks it in two. While suffering the loss of a loved object the melancholy people lose themselves, they become prisoners of distressing emotions. The Thing (or the *other*) inscribed in their memory recurs obsessively and torments the mind. "The thing like the self is a downfall that carries them along into the invisible and unnameable" (15).

This inseparability from one's consciousness is a frequent subject in Dickinson's work. Poem 642 illustrates a subject that cannot escape from the critical judgement of the mind.

> Me from Myself – to banish –
> Had I Art –
> Impregnable my Fortress
> Unto All Heart (Dickinson 318)

The lyrical "I" is divided and multiple. Its own *other* is attacking the mind. It is nagging forcefully and not allowing any rest. The subject would like to be as strong as a fortress and protect oneself but the body is weak and vulnerable.

> But since Myself – assault Me –
> How have I peace
> Except by subjugating
> Consciousness? (Dickinson 318)

The pressure the mind exerts on the self is unbearable and the only way to silence it is to suppress it. The speaker, just like each depressed person, seems to be trapped in a painful situation. She is afraid of losing the *thing* and the loneliness that would follow – as expressed in poem 236. "If He dissolve – then-there is nothing-more- / Eclipse – at Midnight –" However, the memory is a tormenting enemy which does not allow any peace. The short sentences imply a big effort with which the speaker expresses her thoughts. The speech appears to be broken and the rhythm disrupted, but the words are precisely chosen.

The love-hate relationship with the *other* can be found in poem 683.

> The Soul unto itself
> Is an imperial friend –
> Or the most agonizing Spy –
> An Enemy – could send – (Dickinson 338)

In *Powers of Horror: An Essay on Abjection* Kristeva says that a speaking being is "always already haunted by the Other" (qtd. in Sielke 44). This statement is strikingly similar to Dickinson's opening line of poem 670: "One need not be a Chamber – To be Haunted" (333). Dickinson writes here about the brain's corridors where the meeting of the self and the other takes place: "Than Unarmed, one's a'self encounter – / In lonesome Place –" The biggest horror surprisingly does not come from outside but from within: "Our self behind ourself, concealed – / Should startle most –" (333). Sielke points in this line to the intentional stretching of grammar and use of the unusual reflexive pronoun to emphasise the multiplicity in one being. Thus, she comments, Dickinson presents "the crisis of the subject as a crisis of representation, a moment at which language fails" (26) or, following Dahlen's interpretation "'Ourself behind ourself, concealed –' [is] the I and its double, another, the ghost which begins to haunt literature in the middle of the last century, that ghost which is the paranoid double of the ego, an omen of silence, of death" (26).

Hatred towards the lost object leads to self-hatred as the sublime *other* diminishes the depressed, who starts thinking she or he is worthless (Kristeva 11). What is more, the narcissistic individuals feel guilty and bad because of the revengeful emotions toward the unattainable *thing.*

> Far from being a hidden attack on the other who is thought to be hostile because he is frustrating, sadness would point to a primitive self – wounded, incomplete, empty. Persons thus affected do not consider themselves wronged but afflicted with a fundamental flaw, a congenital deficiency. Their sorrow doesn't conceal the guilt or sin felt because of having secretly plotted a revenge on the ambivalent object (Kristeva 12).

This psychoanalytic observation may be useful when trying to decode some of Emily Dickinson's poems. The feeling of guilt is a theme of poem 744.

> Remorse – is Memory – awake -
> Her Parties all astir –
> (...)
> Remorse is cureless – the Disease
> Not even God – can heal –
> For 'tis His institution – and
> The Adequate of Hell – (Dickinson 365)

The poet stresses here the inability to free herself from the feeling of regret, which became the heaviest burden. The relentless thoughts are like an incurable disease which is "The Adequate of Hell." Because the speaker has no control over the wrongdoing, she cherishes no hope for God's forgiveness.

Similarly oppressive is the sorrow in poem 753.

> My soul – accused me – And I quailed –
> As Tongues of Diamond had reviled
> All else accused me – and I smiled -
> My Soul – that Morning – was My friend –
> Her favor – is the best Disdain
> Toward Artifice of Time – or Men (Dickinson 369)

The soul again levels a charge against the speaker. But despite being the judge, the soul is also a friend, probably because it understands the complexity of life. Even though the speaker quails in moments of depression, in high spirits she is able to see the duplicity ("Artifice") of other people and of nature (the "Time"), which justifies her unfriendly feelings. Perhaps she has a right to feel hurt and offended. Dickinson may be oscillating here between accusation and rationalisation of her own action. Sielke comments on the poet's mood swings.

> Dickinson verse delineates various psychic and physical states – conditions that are rarely stable, but rather subjected to sudden changes. Dickinson's 'Delinquent Palaces' (J 959) are conquered in one moment, lost in the next. 'High' and 'low' spirits, gains and losses, pains and powers are dynamic processes within a wide-ranging consciousness (25).

Apart from evoking the sense of guilt the *other* becomes a "tyrannical judge" (Kristeva 11). Through the process of idealisation the lost Thing becomes elevated to the point of worshiping. Confronted with this extolled *thing* the depressive subject demeans oneself and feels worthless, which is destructive to the developing subjectivity. In *Powers of Horror* Kristeva draws attention to the fact that it is especially difficult for women to abject – to let go of the maternal function as they identify with the maternal body as women (Ritzer 424).

> Knowingly disinherited of the *thing,* the depressed person wanders in pursuit of continuously disappointing adventures and loves; or else retreats, disconsolate and aphasic, alone with the unnamed Thing (Kristeva 13).

This notion is best observable in Emily Dickinson's "Master" letters. Due to insufficient evidence concerning the addressee, the letters have kept scholars and readers intrigued for years. There were attempts to identify the "Master" as Samuel Bowles, Charles Wadsworth, T.W. Higginson, and even God. Ruth Owen Jones mentions William Clark, a neighbour and Austin's classmates as an alleged recipient of the letters. Some scholars went as far as to suggest that Emily addresses in the letters her own creativeness. However, even though the identity of "Master" has drawn much attention, it is the language and emotions expressed in the letters that are of prominent importance. Swept by crushing feelings the proud poet tends to glorify the "Master" and decrease her own worth by employing a self-deprecating language. The letters are "written from the point of a little girl who is pleading for acceptance" (Martin, *The Cambridge Introduction to Emily Dickinson* 79). In the first letter the poet writes:

> I wish that I were great, like Mr Angelo, and could paint for you. You ask me what my flowers said – then they were disobedient – I gave them messages. They said what the lips in the West, say, when the sun goes down, and so says the Dawn... Each Sabbath on the Sea, makes me count the Sabbaths, till we meet on shore... I cannot talk any more tonight, for this pain denies me" (qtd. in Martin 79).

Though this letter is more optimistic than the others, here, too, Dickinson uses a self- debasing manner of speech. By comparing herself to "Mr Angelo" she shows her own smallness and doubts her own abilities. Her insignificance and lack of authority is confirmed by the disobedience of the flowers, which did not, deliver the message to the "Master," still they said he was her sun. By using the image of the mighty sun moving across the horizon and a delicate flower-daisy following its way, the poet illustrates the admiration and devotion of a subservient woman for a dominant and powerful man. Such an image, although very romantic, scares the poet, who realizes that dedication means dependence and submissiveness. Tempted by its beauty, intense worshipping jeopardizes the poet's autonomy (Martin, *The Cambridge Introduction to Emily Dickinson*, 81). Defeated by longing and pain the poet cannot write anymore.

In the second "Master" letter the poet appears to be even more fragile and vulnerable. She starts by presenting herself as a wounded bird "If you saw a bullet hit a Bird – and he told you he wasn't shot – you might weep at his courtesy, but you would certainly doubt his word" (Wolff 408). The image of a bird hit with a bullet implies that the denial of pain was just an act of politeness. The voice of a small helpless girl can be heard in the line "Daisy's arm is small – and you have felt the horizon hav'nt you" (408). Dickinson is not oblivious to the fact that the "Master" has absolute power over her and that he does not return her feelings, yet she is unable to escape his charm and his dominance. Feeling so trapped she sees her smallness and frailty.

All the letters support Kristeva's theory that women "have trouble entering the symbolic order because, to do so, they must deny maternal identification – that is, abject themselves" (Hogue 53). What is most interesting in the "Master" letters is that the rebellious by nature poet is trapped in the frames of a socially sanctioned feminine position and cannot overcome the limitation. Even though she tries to reject identification with her weak mother, she repeats her fate, for she finds no alternative for the conventional feminine status. In her attempt to be an object of desire she abnegates herself and becomes not a stronger but a weaker person. Her self-worth drops as she becomes dependent on the man who does not love her. As a result she sinks into "a broken, melancholy language that is symptomatic of the narcissistic crisis" (53). All that she says becomes more and more incoherent. And although according to Kristeva the same subject and speech can bring into being sublimation, which keeps the abject under control, such process does not occur in the "Master" letters. They are saturated with self-abjection (53).

Troubled by the feeling of guilt and in pursuit of the *thing* Dickinson's speaker is often placed "at the edge of subjectivity and representation"

(Sielke 44). Such a "threshold positioning" (44) situates the lyrical "I" on the verge between reality and consciousness, eternity and mortality, subjectivity and representation. These edges are not stages in time but painful processes of border-crossing (44). Overwhelmed by the sorrow of bereavement, the poet, just like Kristeva, understood that a subject's autonomy was dependent on the successful act of separation and liberation from the *other*. In poem 268 the poet writes "Me, change! Me, alter!" (Dickinson 268). The mighty voice accentuated with exclamation marks calls for a different Emily Dickinson – independent, self-assured and with defined objectives in life.

Kristeva calls this process of achieving autonomy a "matricide" – a successful separation from the maternal body. She states that matricide is a prerequisite to our individuation. Unlike the depressive subjects, who in order to protect the mother kill themselves, healthy persons must lose their mother – the *thing* in order to find themselves. This process is done through speech, eroticization of the object and sublimation.

> (...) it is transposed by means of unbelievable symbolic effort, the advent of which one can only admire, which eroticizes the other (the other sex, in the case of the heterosexual woman) or transforms cultural constructs into a "sublime" erotic object (one thinks of the cathexes, by men and women, in social bonds, intellectual and aesthetic productions, etc.) (Kristeva 28).

The new, matured and independent Emily Dickinson found her direction, she transformed the *thing* into her artistic output, which brought her satisfaction and ensured immortality. She expressed her creed in poem 1365.

> Take all away –
> The only thing worth larceny
> Is left– the Immortality – (Dickinson 588)

The immortality that Emily Dickinson dreamed of was not the fame of a historical person. She immortalized herself through the process of creation. Her immortality was the poetic texts which became her symbolic biography. Kristeva notes: "Isn't the artist's life considered, by himself to start with, to be a work of art?" (Kristeva 130).

2.2. Semiotic features in Emily Dickinson's poetic language

In her analysis of different discourses Kristeva pays a lot of attention to poetic language. She refuses to look at it as an "ornament" or "anomalous" action but considers it a "social practice" deserving special attention, particularly with regard to the text's articulation and its explicit message (French, Lack 26). Poetic language reveals the dynamic processes through which signs change their signification as well as show the infiniteness of the whole system of language. She states that "it breaks the inertia of language-habits and offers the linguist a unique opportunity to study the becoming of signification of signs" (28).

Kristeva's main contribution to post-structuralist critique is her distinction between two heterogeneous elements in signification: the semiotic and the symbolic. The symbolic element is associated with structure and grammar. It is what correlates words with meaning and makes references possible. The Symbolic is the Law of the Father which enables the child's entry into language and society. It is that aspect of signification that allows us to take positions and make judgments (Oliver 110).

The semiotic is the way in which bodily drives find their way into language. It refers to an emotional field of instincts and is associated with rhythms, stress and intonation. Deriving from the pre-oedipal stage, this phenomenon is closely connected to the feminine and the maternal. The semiotic elements do not signify but nevertheless "speak." Kristeva describes their meaning as "translinguistic" or "monolinguistic." In other words they cannot be reduced to the symbolic element of language. They give signification in a broader sense. Without them, symbols would be empty and have no importance. Both elements are necessary for signification and there is continuous fluctuation between them. Without the symbolic, speech would not make sense, it would be delirium. Without semiotic we would have empty utterances (Oliver 110).

According to Kristeva, poetic language allows most space for the semiotic. Rhythm, rhymes, intonation, alliteration, word-play are all demonstrations of bodily drives. Interestingly, Kristeva draws an analogy between the language of poetry and the speech of a melancholy person. In both cases there is a return to the origins of language (Smith, *Julia Kristeva: Speaking the Unspeakable* 40). As a sort of "pre-symbolic signification" these maternal energies "manifest themselves in syntactic disruptions and semantic incoherence. Moving at the margins of discourse, the semiotic foregrounds the heterogeneity and materiality of a text while destabilising its meaning. Due to this return of the body in language, the subject can no longer be understood as a fixed entity" (Sielke 23).

In *Black Sun* Kristeva defines the speech of a depressive person, who gripped by pain and hopelessness sinks into the "blackness of asymbolia" (33) and communicates emotions on the semiotic level. Inconsolable despair hinders the sequence of a language code. The utterances become illogical, interrupted and often come to a standstill. Conceptual retardation, which is one of the features of melancholy, renders the speech sluggish, repetitious and often changes it into "obsessive litanies" (33). Kristeva recognizes a pattern that differentiates the depressive discourse:

> Speech delivery is slow, silences are long and frequent, rhythm slacken, intonation becomes monotonous, and the very syntactic structures – without evidencing disturbances and disorders such as can be observed in schizophrenics – are often characterized by nonrecoverable elisions (34).

Smith, following Kristeva's concept, observes that the reader or listener of both poetry and a melancholy speech is confronted with a new mysterious language whose meaning is concealed and often incomprehensible (40).

This analysis of Emily Dickinson's verse will attempt to show how the semiotic undermines the symbolic and how the clinical symptoms filter through her texts. Applying Kristeva's category of semiotic features in poetic language this section will also present a catalogue of depressive characteristics which Dickinson displays in her poetry. As determined by Kristeva the most frequent ways in which semiotics penetrate into the text are: "unorderable cognitive chaos" (33), compression and elisions, absurd phrases, alliteration, punctuation, slow delivery, mood swings and interrupted phrases . All of these factors are traits of a depressive state and hint at the difficulty in concatenation. They are also responsible for causing ambiguity and obstructing interpretation (33–34). Each of these will be illustrated below.

2.2.1. "Unorderable cognitive chaos"

The first observation which indicates that Dickinson's texts are waves of semiotic discharge is that her poetry is founded on creative chaos. Her poems were neither dated nor titled. There was no design to them. Porter observed that we "have in Dickinson not order but restlessness" (7). Her poetry is of great strength but lacking direction. In one of her letters the poet admitted herself: "I hardly know what I have said" and continued: "My words put all their feathers on – and flutter here and there" (qtd. in Porter 110). In another letter she complains about the lack of control over her creative urge: "I had no Monarch in my life and cannot rule myself, when I try to organise – my little Force explodes – and leaves me bare and charred" (qtd. in Porter 111). In connection with this we can formulate a general hypothesis that Dickinson texts are saturated with maternal energies. In Kristeva's theory the discharge of emotions – a specific flow of expression – is more important than being understood by the listener. Dickinson obsessively puts across her creative need. One can risk a statement that Dickinson's poetry is founded on a semiotic pattern of poetic language. In almost all of her texts the semiotic outweighs the symbolic.

2.2.2. Ambiguity caused by compression and elision

Perhaps no other poet used such extreme economy of writing as Emily Dickinson. She used her own hermetic language, often impenetrable to readers. Cristanne Miller observes that Emily Dickinson's cryptic and intangible poems

> (...) baffle even sophisticated readers. Her poetry is elliptically compressed, disjunctive, at times ungrammatical; its reference is unclear; its metaphors are so densely compacted that literal components of meaning fade... One of the difficulties is to understand the tension between the poet's desire to speak to an audience and her decision to write the riddling elliptical poetry she does (Miller 1).

The most frequent devices causing difficulties in interpretation are deletions. These equivalents of depressive silences are present in almost every poem. In order to understand the text one must reinstate what is absent. But while ellipses of function words can be easily restored, non-recoverable elisions are just silences open to interpretation. This, however, means that all we can say about a certain text is hypothetical.

Critics of literature have deciphered poem 102 as a letter to her brother, Austin.

> Great Caesar! Condescend
> The Daisy, to receive,
> Gathered by Cato's Daughter,
> With your majestic leave! (Dickinson 50)

Elizabeth Petrino interprets this verse as the poet's playful plea to be admitted into Caesar's (Austin's) presence. Dickinson who presents herself as Daisy and Cato – Caesar's opponent's daughter, offers him a flower as a gesture of reconciliation (156). It is one possible proposition, but the text alone, without specific context, remains enigmatic for the contemporary reader, unaware of biographical details. Most, if not all, of Dickinson's texts are connected with biographical elements, but the semiotic intrusion obscures the message, often making them undecipherable. Extreme deletions have concealed the meaning of the poem 483. The first line seems not to make any sense: "A Wonderful – to feel the Sun?". It is only through the effort of the reader that the silences gain significance. Using the hints that are further on in the poem Porter reconstitutes the line to its full form: "It is a wonderful thing within the Soul to feel the Sun" (43). Here Dickinson deleted not only single words but the entire phrase "thing within the Soul." Thus, in this single line, six words contain the meaning of twelve (43).

Another expressive example of a text which has its syntax disturbed by a flow of semiotic discharge is poem 819.

All I may, if small,
Do it not display
Larger for the Totalness –
'Tis Economy

To bestow a World
And withhold a Star –
Utmost, is Munificence –
Less, tho' larger, poor (Dickinson 398)

The first line is characterized by non-recoverable deletions. We can assume a lot of different endings of both phrases. "All I may, if small" – this statement may be completed by different verbs. All I may... do, think, receive? The question remains unanswered. The inconclusiveness is enhanced by grammatical incorrectness in the second line. If the expression "Do it" is an order, then it should have been marked by a comma (Do it,) and the rest of the line should contain an auxiliary verb "do" (do not display). The symbolic order seems completely destabilised. The remaining two lines are equally puzzling due to further elisions and perplexing language. The poet uses too general, abstract concepts for the reader to be able to catch the broad sense of the verse. Similarly challenging is the second stanza. The phrase: "To bestow a World" lacks an object. The words in the last line "less," "larger," "poor" are in opposition to each other and introduce a sort of a tension. Loss of clarity of mind, doubt, and an undefined sense of anxiety are all traces of the depressive state.

2.2.3. Unorthodox treatment of grammar

Unconventional use of grammar causes a lot of confusion among Emily Dickinson's readers. She ignores the traditional rules and invents her special language code governed by emotions rather than regulations. Her uncurbed language mode displays flawed syntax, unusual word capitalization, very complex metaphors and an unorthodox use of punctuation.

Poem 466 is an example of verse which totally disregards the conventional language rules.

'Tis little I – could care for Pearls –
Who own the ample sea –
Or Brooches – when the Emperor –
With Rubies – pelteth me –

Or Gold- who am the Prince of Mines –
Or Diamonds – when have I
A Diadem to fit a Dome –
Continual upon me – (Dickinson 224)

The text lacks a natural flow; the phrases do not seem connected due to elisions and a changed word order. For instance the inversion "have I/ A Diadem to fit a Dome –" suggests a question, but it is not. Instead of commas or full stops Dickinson uses only dashes. They introduce silences which serve as pauses between broken utterances. There are no dots which would signify the end of one thought and the beginning of another; instead we have one flow of fragmented utterances. In addition, the poet capitalizes some nouns according to the emotional weight they carry for her. On the whole looking at the poem from Kristeva's perspective it is easy to notice the uncontrolled inner energies coming to light.

The lack of compliance to grammatical rules or design is evident in poem 480.

"Why do I love" You, Sir?
Because –
The Wind does not require the Grass
To answer – Wherefore when He pass
She cannot keep Her place.

Because He knows – and
Do not You
And We know not –
Enough for Us
The Wisdom it be so – (Dickinson 231)

The poet drops the "s" with some verbs and applies it to others. In the same random way Dickinson also assigns gender to some nouns; she does it to wind, grass, lightning and sunrise, but not to the eye. The wind and lightning become "He," grass "She," but the eye keeps its regular form "it" (Porter 49). The second stanza is very distinctive for changed word order: "Do not You" (You do not), and "We know not" (we do not know).

Another problem in decoding the poems is the blurred distinction between the active and the passive voice. Having compared poem 524 with its double version Porter suggests that when the poet wrote "Great Clouds-like Ushers-leaning" she actually meant that "the Great Clouds *were placed*," so the active voice was used in place of the passive one. This pattern also occurs also in poem 594, where Dickinson writes about the Soul's battle: "Its bodiless Campaign / Establishes, and terminates." What should have been written is: "Its bodiless Campaign / *Is* established and terminates" (Porter 53). Finally another frequent grammatical defect is changes in reflexive pronouns. For example in poem 417 we read:

> "Homesick"? Many met it –
> Even through them – This
> Cannot testify –
> Themself – as dumb – (Dickinson 199)

"Themselves" was altered to "themself" as if the poet wanted to reduce the *many* to one. The intensity of feelings experienced by one is as powerful as the emotions of many.

2.2.4. Absurd phrases

The next feature of the semiotic order is absurd phrases caused by the inadequacy of the symbolic order. When signs are loaded with affect they become ambiguous, and often nonsensical (Kristeva 42). Absurd utterances are commonplace in Emily Dickinson's poetry. Just as the poet withdrew from reality, so did her poems. As an example of the oddness of her lexicon Porter cites some phrases from her letters. In one of them she wrote: "I can murmur broken," in a different one: "To scan a Ghost, is faint" (52). Equally abnormal is the poet's choice of adjectives in her verse. In poem 88 we find "Penurious eyes," in 414 "delirious hem" and poem 465 talks about "stumbling buzz." Many of her poems can be read only with the help of her private code, which can be established after analysing similarities in her poems (Porter 56).

However, for an average reader the majority of her poems will remain inaccessible and intriguing. One such text is poem 16.

> I would distill a cup,
> And bear to all my friends,
> Drinking to her no more astir,
> By beck, or burn, or moor! (Dickinson 13)

Even though the whole verse is of a mysterious character, the last line seems especially absurd. All of these words indicate completely different semantic pools and it is difficult to determine any connection between them.

Further confusion is brought by the absence of reference. The poet repeatedly uses an unassigned "it" and although it adds to the establishment of intimacy it also introduces an unidentifiable world into the verse (Porter 54). For instance in poem 560 we are at a loss as to who or what hides behind the secretive "It."

It knew no lapse, nor Diminution –
But large – serene –
Burned on – until through Dissolution –
It failed from Men – (Dickinson 272)

The lack of a subject and a specific, tangible reality also points to the predominance of emotions over actual events. The phrases are so abstract that they sound totally absurd.

2.2.5. Slow delivery

Melancholy people submerged in affect produce a new kind of language. Helplessness and despair lead them to inaction and language retardation. Life loses meaning and speech its vitality and clarity. The retarded or fatigued speech gives the melancholy person a distorted sense of time. They do not remember the past nor can they plan for the future: "Time does not pass by, the before / after notion does not rule it, does not direct it from a past toward a goal" (Kristeva 60). Dickinson expressed it in poem 650.

Pain – has an Element of Blank –
It cannot recollect
When it begun – or if there were
A time when it was not – (Dickinson 323)

As life has lost its meaning and time is not important, the depressive speech is slow and monotonous. The effect of slow delivery is achieved by the use of repetitive structures. Poem 692 captures the moment of dying.

The Sun kept setting – setting – still (stanza 1)
The Dusk kept dropping – dropping – still (stanza 2)
My Feet kept drowsing – drowsing – still (stanza 3) (Dickinson 341)

The repetition sets up a special, lethargic mood in this poem. Everything seems to be happening in slow motion. The fading of existence is accompanied by a sense of serenity and acceptance.

2.2.6. Repetition and obsessive litanies

The speech of melancholy people is musical, alliterative and repetitive. According to Kristeva's theory it results from the subject's effort to convey the "noncommunicable" or the fixation on the lost *thing*. There are different types of repetition in Emily Dickinson's poems: repetition of phrases, parallels of syntax, repetition of the same sound and alliterations.

2.2.6.1. Repetition of a phrase

Poem 536 is one of the many examples of a repetitive phrase.

> The Heart asks Pleasure – first –
> And then – Excuse from Pain –
> And then – those little Anodynes
> That deaden suffering –
>
> And then – to go to sleep –
> And then – if it should be
> The will of its Inquisitor
> The privilege to die – (Dickinson 262)

The phrase "And then" is uttered almost mechanically, without much consideration. The speaker does not seem to concentrate on the sophistication of delivery, but communicates the message spontaneously, as if in one surge of energy.

2.2.6.2. Parallels of syntax

In poem 640 a few verses repeat the same order or grammatical structures.

> "I cannot live with You –" (stanza 1)
> "I could not die – with You –" (stanza 4)
> "Nor could I rise – with You –" (stanza 6) (Dickinson 317)

This type of repetition provides the poem with melody and it makes the verse more memorable. However, it can also indicate the subject's compulsive preoccupation with a certain idea.

2.2.6.3. Repetition of the same sound and alliteration

The first stanza of poem 1071 begins with the same consonant.

> Perception of an object costs
> Precise the Object's loss
> Perception in itself a Gain
> Replying to its Price – (Dickinson 486)

The poem appears an emotive warning against jumping to a conclusion when estimating something. Our wrong opinion may reduce the value of an object or ruin it. Through the repetition of the sound "p" the poem becomes distinctive. The plosive consonant starts each line with some pressure which is gradually released as the lines come to an end. This way the poem is loaded with affect. What also draws attention is the design of the verse – that is the sound "p" starts three successive lines and then the concluding word of the stanza. It looks as if an established order took a sudden shift. Although the word "Price" may be considered as a part of a frame, the balance of the stanza is definitely disturbed.

Repetition of different sound patterns is a very frequent occurrence in Dickinson's poems. Bloom and Priddy explain that the poets alliteration results from her attempt to draw importance to some words. For instance poem 1129, beginning with the line "Tell all the Truth but tell it slant," emphasises the sound "t" and "s" because the whole poem is based on the concept of "truth" and "circuit" (246). Kristeva's theory, however, points to alliteration as one of the depressive features. The sound "s" and "t" are again alliterated in poem 686 which says that "suffering strengthens" and "Time is a Test of Trouble –" (Dickinson 339) Interpreting alliteration as a mark of the semiotic, one can read the repetition of sounds as a sort of a depressive chant.

2.2.6.4. Obsessive litanies

Sometimes the lines of a poem appear to be spoken in the same breath. The flow of utterances changes into what Kristeva calls "obsessive litanies" (33). In poem 639 Dickinson builds an image of the gruesome Civil War.

> 'This populous with Bone and stain –
> And Men too straight to stoop again,
> And Piles of solid Moan –
> And Chips of Blank – in Boyish Eyes –
> And scraps of Prayer –
> And Death's surprise,
> Stamped visible – in Stone – (Dickinson 316)

This middle stanza contrasts with the first and last one through its graphic image. Judy Small notes that while the other stanzas are pensive and meditative the middle one illustrates the real horror of the war. The difference is also marked by the change in rhymes. The partially rhymed outer stanzas are outweighed by the full rhyme in the two opening lines of the central one and the ominous relationship between the words "Moan" and "Stone" (97). The recurring "And" betrays a highly distressed speaker bombarded with sinister views of the war.

2.2.7. Interruption in speech flow

An example of Kristeva's notion of depressive, broken speech which comes to an abrupt halt is poem 280. In the last stanza the poet describes her own death as plunging into the unknown. Her heart-breaking account, slowed down by commas, dashes and repetitions suddenly breaks as if gripped by overpowering sadness or dread.

> And then a Plank in Reason, broke,
> And I dropped down, and down –
> And hit a World, at every plunge,
> And Finished knowing – then – (Dickinson 129)

The final word "then" gains even more substance by the fact that it is separated with dashes. The first dash implies that the word "then" was not a spontaneous one; the speaker hesitated or was running out of energy. The second hyphen is an indication that the subject stopped signifying and sunk into the silence of grief.

Not a dramatic pause but a break of the continuity of thought characterises poem 1107. According to Porter the last line, instead of completing the poem, diverts into inconclusiveness (109).

> From Heavy laden Lands to thee
> Were seas to cross to come
> A Caspian were crowded –
> Too near thou art for Fame – (Dickinson 499)

Porter comments on the poet's lack of consistency:

> It seems that Dickinson brought the poem to a close without the mold of a clear idea of what the poem was to say in its totality. It ends short of completion, the result of writing cut loose from discipline and the challenge and check of a design (109).

These sudden breaks and changes in thought directions indicate lack of organisation and control. The texts are a flow of intense emotions. Porter compares them to impressionist music where despite an effort the resolving sound is never found (110).

2.2.8. The pressure for silence

When considering silence in Emily Dickinson's poetic texts, two of Kristeva's observations gain significance. The first one is that the depressive person is a "prisoner of affect" (14). The psychomotor and ideational retardation are responsible for hindering the regular pace of speech. And the second is that melancholy people become thinkers: "In his doubtful moments the depressed person is a philosopher" (6). In both cases the unspoken carries as much meaning as the words themselves. The most common way in which Emily Dickinson achieves silence in her poetry is the use of dashes. She adopts this practice to present the moment when the subject is too moved to speak fluently, to construct pathos and to stress some words of wisdom. Poem 196 talks about one of the most difficult experiences of human existence – death. In the last two stanzas, which are the most touching, she separates almost every word with a dash.

> We must die – by and by –
> Clergymen say –
> Tim – shall – if I – do –
> I – too – if he –
>
> How shall we arrange it –
> Tim – was – so – shy?
> Take us simultaneous – Lord –
> I – "Tim" – and – Me! (Dickinson 93)

Dashes help here to illustrate the unutterable grief. If written in a normal way the verse would not be so powerful. The lines seem broken, just like the subject's existence. The hyphens in this poem may represent sobs or a state of mental numbness. But when in another text Dickinson affirms "Truth – is as old as Gold –" Doriani suggests that the poet employs the practice that *Rhetorical Reader* and other homiletical rhetoric books recommend. Using pauses helps to establish a tone of solemnity and "give weight to a good thought" (48). The dash often creates silence to draw the audience's attention and allow space for philosophical thought.

2.2.9. Mood swings – self belittling to self-confidence

One of the symptoms of depression is mood disorder. Mood swings are characterized by periods of depression and mania. During the episodes of depression the melancholy person may experience sadness, emptiness, feelings of guilt and worthlessness.

> Denial [of negation of loss] annihilates even the introjections of depressive persons and leaves them with the feeling of being worthless, "empty." By belittling and destroying themselves, they exhaust any possibility of an object, and this is also a roundabout way of preserving it... elsewhere, untouchable (Kristeva 48).

The "Master" letters, discussed previously are the best example of self-degradation. Their language is so self-abnegating that they betray total submissiveness and worthlessness. Cynthia Wolff observes that when the poet outlines her feelings, language of poetry takes over and changes the epistolary prose style into a lyrical one (408). This comment supports Kristeva's theory about the poetic language allowing most space for the semiotic.

Another example of belittling is poem 486, whose tone borders on self-pity.

I was the slightest in the House –
I took the smallest Room –
(...)
I never spoke – unless addressed –
And then, 'twas brief and law – (Dickinson 234)

The poem portrays a quiet, unimportant woman of petite posture. By saying that she occupied the smallest room she implies that she was not respected much, even in her own home. Her admission that she spoke only when asked exhibits dependence and obedience. Such an image of herself could only have been outlined during moments of deep dejection.

The predisposition to depressive moods and self-belittling is also explicit in poem 146, in which she describes herself as a little, meaningless figure.

On such a night, or such a night,
Would anybody care
If such a little figure
Slipped quiet from its chair – (Dickinson 69)

Gripped by a sense of severe anxiety the poet is having suicidal thoughts. Her self-esteem is so low that she wonders if anyone would miss her if she suddenly died.

According to Kristeva the opposing strategy to diminishing is "stimulation and reinforcement" which can be achieved by means of language. Speech as a carrier of desires has an activating effect on the neurobiological network (36). In her explanation of how the language operates Kristeva compares the depressive subject to a child learning how to speak.

> (...) unlike animals whose only recourse is in behaviour, the child can find... solution in psychic representation and in language. The child imagines, thinks out, utters...and this can be a deterrent from withdrawal into inactivity or playing dead, wounded by irreparable frustration or harm (36).

This surge of life force, stimulated by language, found its reflection in the already mentioned poem 528. The repetition of the capitalized word "Mine" shows a powerful moment in the life of the depressive subject. The mood of the poem is intensified by exclamation marks. The speaker is no longer a silent, obedient figure. Her voice is mighty and demanding.

Mine – by the Right of the White Election!
Mine – by the Royal Seal!
Mine – by the Sign in the Scarlet prison –
Bars – cannot conceal! (Dickinson 258)

The authors of *Dickinson and Audience* note that the poem can be read as "an affirmation of self, which chooses its own kind of ascendancy by its own terms" (Orzeck, Weisbuch 53).

Poem 431 is another powerful, exclamatory verse.

> Me – come! My dazzled face
> In such a shiny place!
> Me – hear! My foreign Ear
> The sounds of Welcome – there! (Dickinson 207)

In her moment of strength the poet seems very excited by the prospect of being admitted into Paradise. Her revived imagination fantasises about the thrills awaiting her in the Promised Land. Again the word "Me" reveals a very confident, assertive speaker. The next part of the poem concentrates on a different sort of immortality – fame.

> The Saints forget
> Our bashful feet –
> My Holiday, shall be
> That They – remember me –
> My Paradise – the fame
> That They – pronounce my name – (Dickinson 207)

The poet emerges here as a positive, goal-oriented individual. Her language becomes a carrier of desires and wishes. She does not seem submerged in depression anymore but is ready for the effort and poetic toil.

In *Black Sun*, while seeking connections between the melancholic mood and language Kristeva observes that:

> Literary creation is that adventure of the body and signs that bears witness to the affect – to sadness as imprint of separation and beginning of the symbol's sway; to joy as imprint of the triumph that settles me in the universe of artifice and symbol, which I try to harmonise in the best possible way with my experience of reality (20).

Kristeva emphasises the healing power of artistic expression. It is through sublimation that one is able to overcome mourning. However, melancholy leaves its traces in every work of art.

The above analysis confirms Kristeva's theory, and shows that the depressive subject reveals itself in a literary text through its semiotic dimension, that is rhythm, pace and all those meanings which remain for the reader unclear or not verbalised. They are all traces of the creative subject's depression which has been overcome in the act of writing.

2.3. Strategies for representing suffering

This section of the thesis is devoted to the interpretative techniques of a work of art proposed by Julia Kristeva. She concentrates on the form to show that the structure corresponds to the symbolic element of language. As a framework is an integral part of a work of art it carries as much significance as its content. The last part of this chapter will illustrate the application of Kristeva's interpretative methods in relation to the poetic texts of Emily Dickinson.

2.3.1. Minimalism as a technique for representing despair

In her interpretation of Holbein's painting *The Body of the Dead Christ in the Tomb*, Kristeva emphasises the concept of artistic minimalism. She claims that minimalism is a technique of representation which intensifies the expression of despair. She comments on Holbein's painting:

> Indeed, his minimalism maintained a powerful, expressive seriousness that one understands readily when one contrasts it with the stately but haughty sadness, one that is incommunicable and somewhat artificial, of the Jansenist *Dead Christ* by the Philippe de Champaigne (126).

Black Sun proposes an analogous understanding of aesthetic minimalism as a strategy for creation and reading of a text – the fewer words, the more possibilities of interpretation. It seems that in Kristeva's theory minimalism conveys the power and intensity of the pain of a depressive subject. The most constructive part of her thesis is the paradox that a source of creativity springs out of anguish.

While interpreting Holbein's work Kristeva focuses not on the literary biography of the depressive artist but on the biography of a depressive subject who is presented in the work of art. Kristeva suggests that minimalism captures a unique "melancholy moment" (128).

> It is not my point to maintain that Holbein was afflicted with melancholia or that he painted melancholy people. More profoundly, it would seem, on the bases of his oeuvre (including his themes and painterly technique), that a *melancholy moment* (an actual or imaginary loss of meaning, an actual or imaginary despair, an actual or imaginary razing of symbolic values, including the value of life) summoned up his aesthetic activity, which overcame the melancholy latency while keeping its trace (128).

According to Kristeva the suffering of the depressive subject, which is visualized in her contemplation of Holbein's painting – his practice of minimalism – is both a theme and a technique of creation. In the light of Kristeva's theory suffering represents "severance" (135), which means that it refers to the formal and symbolic dimension of a work of art.

One of the characteristics of minimalism Dickinson applies is compression. She uses this literary device to create density and compactness of both themes and forms. Crucial themes of human existence are condensed into very short texts. Despair, agony, love death and loneliness are usually illustrated through dynamic, poetic images and incisive rhetorical phrases.

Poem 1243 is an example of great existential themes condensed into dynamic poetic images.

> Safe Despair it is that raves –
> Agony is frugal.
> Puts itself severe away
> For its own perusal
>
> Garrisoned no Soul can be
> In the Front of Trouble –
> Love is one, not aggregate –
> Nor is Dying double (Dickinson 546)

Dickinson creates an opposition of two notions which are illustrated by allegory: Despair and Agony. Paradoxically, the Despair is associated with safety because it has the possibility of being expressed through "raves." In this way Despair is an image of an act of speech which is verbalised and thus, using Kristeva's hypothesis, prevents a melancholy withdrawal (36). It is in opposition to Agony, which by being an analogue of silence, points to a depressive stupor. This dichotomy of Despair and Agony corresponds to the duality of existence and death. "Agony is frugal/ Puts itself severe away." In the second stanza appears another allegorical pair: Love and Dying. Both point to minimalism and the condensation of the huge theme of loneliness. Love and Dying are the same experience of a single "Soul." For Dickinson the confrontation with primary themes of human existence is a sign of fear with no support from another person: "Garrisoned no Soul can be/ In the Front of Trouble –". The dash finishing the line is the most dramatic conclusion of Dickinson's thought. It creates suspense and compels the reader's contemplation. Neither Love nor Dying are capable of creating durable human bonds, which give the feeling of safety. As a consequence man is always single and lonely: "Love is one, not aggregate – / Nor is Dying double." The minimalism of this statement is characteristic of Dickinson's style of writing.

Another example of Dickinson's tendency to minimalist writing is a short text which, despite its simplicity, could be a treatise about human destiny.

In this short Life
That only lasts an hour
How much – how little – is
Within our power (Dickinson 562)

Simplicity of form – simple rhymes, straightforward words – contrasts with the massive subject matter. The essential and ironic style of Dickinson poems is most visible in their shortest forms.

The technique of poetic minimalism in Dickinson's creative strategy is connected with a variety of possible interpretations. The fewer words she uses the more capacity they have and the more weight they carry. The finest examples of this poetic practice are poems with two lines, which can be considered Dickinson's words of wisdom. They often take the form of a question or an imperative. These grammatical forms add to the power of minimalism making it an even more efficient way of emotional expression. Here is one of several examples of this rule – poem 1728.

Is Immortality a bane –
The men are so oppressed? (Dickinson 701)

Immortality is connected with three key words: bane, men, oppressed, which reveal the pain as a poetic suffering. The compression of the words results in the difficulty of decoding the meaning. Reading the poem becomes a painful process of deciphering. In this way the method of interpretation is a continuation of the creation technique.

A difficult puzzle for decoding is poem 1095.

To Whom the Mornings stand for Nights,
What must the Midnights – be! (Dickinson 495)

One can risk a statement that this poem constitutes the most minimalistic and essential definition of a depressive subject. Through economical use of words Dickinson illustrates the depth of human despair, or putting it in Kristeva's words, she presents "a darkness without hope, a recession of perspective, including that of life" (133). Dickinson conveys with mastery, what for a depressive subject is non-communicable – the sorrow connected with existential themes of the human condition.

2.3.2. Composition as a technique to present loneliness

'Father, why have you deserted me?' (qtd. in Kristeva 133)

In further analysis of Holbein's work, Kristeva points to separation as one of the key components to illustrate the depth of suffering. While Italian artists were inclined to present the Saviour during the Passion surrounded by people, the German painter presents Christ in complete isolation. The tormented body lies stretched out away from people and forgotten by the Father. Such an empty form, presenting suffering devoid of any compassion, enhances the effect of human misery. Kristeva notes:

> It is perhaps that isolation – an act of composition – that endows the painting with its major melancholy burden, more so than delineation and colouring... such realism, harrowing on account of its very parsimony, is emphasized to the utmost through the painting's composition and location: a body stretched out alone, situated above the viewers, and separated from them (113).

Holbein's arrangement of the picture emphasises terrifying human loneliness. All the worse, deprived also of any hope for the beyond. Christ, just like people, is subject to the laws of nature and abandoned by the Father.

Isolation is not only a theme but also a setting in Emily Dickinson's poetry. Human drama appears to be happening in a timeless void and total seclusions. Her speakers are often isolated from their family, audience and even God. She writes about poets – martyrs who do not share their pain with anyone, about separated lovers and those who are losing their mind and become strangers even to themselves. In the previous chapter we attempted to present how this loneliness permeates Emily Dickinson's poems. Now we would like to focus on the way the sense of isolation is communicated.

One of the methods used to create a timeless, desolate abyss as a background is to describe silence as difficult to endure. Poem 1004 is an example of this technique.

> There is no Silence in the Earth – so silent
> As that endured
> Which uttered, would discourage Nature
> And haunt the World. (Dickinson 465)

Silence, which is usually associated with relaxation, becomes synonymous with an agonising solitude. Only silence marked by the absence of close ones can be really "silent," when pain is not alleviated by anyone's solace. Such silence has the power to torment the mind. In poem 1251 the speaker says: "Silence is all we dread" (548).

Sometimes silence and isolation are not named but achieved by creating a special atmosphere, as in poem 465.

> I heard a Fly buzz – when I died –
> The Stillness in the Room
> Was like the Stillness in the Air –
> Between The Heaves of Storm (Dickinson 223)

The image of the flying fly evokes a sensation of silence, as only in stillness can the buzz become so distinctive. It also conveys an atmosphere of emptiness and a mental detachment. There are people in the room, as the speaker says that there are "Eyes around" and "Breaths were gathering firm," but there is no sign of an emotional bond between the speaker and the mourners. There are no tears, no goodbye speeches on the part of the watchers or sentiments on the part of the dying person. The buzzing fly becomes a sign of solitude and the meaninglessness of human existence.

Emily Dickinson also uses such graphic rendering of isolation in poem 280. A funeral, which represents the death of her mind, serves as a background to illustrate alienation between people. The mourners are anonymous and faceless and again no words are spoken or tears shed. Through the use of repetitive words, the ritualistic actions they perform seem automatic and dehumanized.

> I felt a Funeral, in my Brain,
> And Mourners to and fro
> Kept treading – treading – till it seemed
> That Sense was breaking through –
> And they all were seated,
> (...)
> And then I heard them lift a Box (Dickinson 128)

The unbridgeable distance between her and the others contributes to the insurmountable despair of the speaker. Realizing her alienation she laments "And I, and Silence, some strange Race / Wrecked, solitary, here –" The mourners who were supposed to be her friends were complete aliens.

There are different types of solitude in Dickinson's work. She writes about solitude triggered by absence, solitude among people but also solitude caused by a lack of faith. In poem 357 she sadly remarks: "God is a distant – Stately Lover –" (169) and in poem 376 she complains that although she prayed, God never really cared: "He cared as much as on the Air/ A Bird – had stamped her foot –" (179) The world deserted by God and people became not only the background for Dickinson's verse, but also for her private life in seclusion.

2.3.3. Sarcasm and irony as a tool to illustrate defiance

As one of the causes of depression is the feeling of being defeated, Kristeva recognizes sarcasm and irony as a response to failure and pain. Mocking smiles of a depressive subject do not express exultation or victory, but are often the last attempt of resistance against the implacable laws of nature. On the example of Holbein's *The Body of the Dead Christ in the Tomb* Kristeva explains:

> Clasped in the arms of Death, no one escapes its grip, a fatal one to be sure, but here anguish conceals its own depressive force and displays defiance through sarcasm or the grimace of a mocking smile, lacking triumphancy, as if, in the knowledge of being done for, laughter was the only answer (118).

According to Kristeva, while Eros's vitality produces an abundance of joyful or eroticized morbid symbols, death calls for minimalism, realism and irony. Irony reflects disappointment and conveys the hideousness of death.

> ... a grating irony: this brings forth the 'danse macabre' and disenchanted profligacy inborn in the painter's style. The self eroticizes and signifies the obsessive presence of Death by stamping with isolation, emptiness, or absurd laughter its own imaginative assurance that keeps it alive, that is, anchored in the interplay of forms (138).

Thanatos, being imprinted in our subconscious, does not allow us to forget the universality of death. Harsh irony and absurd laughter find their expression in an artist's work as a representation of deathly drives and they indicate realization of the fragility of life.

While Dickinson's use of irony is often regarded as amusing, following the theory of Kristeva, we will argue that most of it was activated by suffering. For a poet who opposed male dominance, rejected conformity and traditional religion, irony was yet another tool to communicate frustration, bitterness and disenchantment with the brutal world. In moments of helplessness it was the only possible response.

Poem 61 seems like one of the earliest examples of this painful humour. The speaker jokingly asks God to consider her among the saved ones.

> Papa above!
> Regard a Mouse
> O'erpowred by the Cat!
> Reserve within thy Kingdom
> A "Mansion" for the Rat! (Dickinson 32)

Dickinson's exaggerated humility – presenting herself as a rat – betrays a strong sarcasm. Her disrespectful tone hints on great sadness resulting from the loss of faith and feeling of worthlessness. Humour and despondency mix also in poem 288 where the poet again addresses her insignificant existence.

> I'm Nobody! Who are you?
> Are you – Nobody – Too?
> Then there's a pair of us!
> Don't tell! They'd advertise – you know! (Dickinson133)

The poem is a biting satire on society and public figures that are in a constant search for self-importance. However, the poem also discloses the poet's doubts about her own self-worth. Angela Conrad comments on Emily Dickinson's ironic style of the two poems mentioned: "Despite her humorous tone, we can see these poems as a youthful rehearsal of later self – deprecation" (59). Both poems in a seemingly funny way touch upon the most serious existential problems of the poet's life – her low self-esteem and loneliness.

The sharpest sarcasm is explicit in poems addressed to the Almighty. Having experienced a great number of losses Emily Dickinson often blames God for cruelty and deception. Poem 1461, which starts with a plea to God and finishes with an accusation, can be read as an inversion of The Lord's Prayer. Disappointed and frustrated with unanswered appeals, in an attempt at defiance, she declaims:

"Heavenly Father" – take to thee
The supreme iniquity
Fashioned by thy candid Hand
In a moment contraband –
Though to trust us – seem to us
More respectful – "We are Dust" –
We apologize to thee
For thine own Duplicity – (Dickinson 619)

God, who was the embodiment of goodness, love and justice, just like people, failed in His greatness. When faith and hope die, then what is left is irony and absurd laughter.

This spasm of laughter, which Kristeva recognizes as a reaction to excruciating pain, is skilfully depicted in poem 410. The poem illustrates the mental breakdown of a speaker who, having experienced a few disasters, cannot cope any longer. Losing sanity she confesses:

My Brain – begun to laugh –
I mumbled – like a fool –
And tho''tis Years ago – that Day –
My Brain keeps giggling – still (Dickinson 195)

Dickinson's mode of irony in poetic texts indicates her vast knowledge of the subject of suffering. She makes us think about the capacity of the human heart and limitations of endurance. Irony is an act of boldness in the face of calamity. Just like a glove thrown down in a challenge, it is a courageous answer given to Death.

2.3.4. Realism as a technique of humanising pain

What also draws Kristeva's special attention in Holbein's painting is realism. While analysing his masterpiece she defines an artistic rule of constructing realism in the process of creation:

> Holbein maintains grief while humanising it, without following the Italian path of negating pain and glorifying the arrogance of the flash or the beauty of the beyond. Holbein belongs in another dimension: he makes commonplace of the Passion of the crucified Christ in order to make it more accessible to us (117).

The French writer singles out Holbein's work for its authenticity and accuracy in portraying details. The life size, unadorned Christ's body, lying in isolation, with his face contorted, conveys the image of real human suffering. Such a realistic depiction brings the notion of pain closer and makes us more familiar with it.

Not many other poets have ever written about pain and death in such detail as Emily Dickinson. In her poems, just like Holbein, Dickinson makes us accustomed to the true look of suffering and passing away. Having participated physically and emotionally in many deaths, she was able to reconstruct in her poems the scenes she witnessed. Her remarkable ability for observation allowed her to present the process of passing away from the point of view of the observer and the dying person.

Death seen through the eyes of the dying person became the theme of two poems mentioned earlier: "I heard a Fly buzz- when I died –" and "I felt a funeral in my brain." In both poems we have an act of dying vividly reconstructed. The first death is very peaceful, disturbed only by a noisy fly. Dickinson masterfully illustrates the atmosphere in the room and the last thoughts of the dying person. Tandon and Trevedi comment on the realism of the depiction: "Here Emily Dickinson attains a degree of 'Negative Capability,' which takes her quite near to the sensations and physical experience of the dying man" (90). The second poem, on the contrary, presents death accompanied by tormenting psychic pain. Scrupulous description of the dying subject's sensations – her irritation with mourners and anxiety caused by the unknown – makes the reader enter the dying person's mind and participate in the final scene of dying.

Poem 547 presents another perspective on death. It is written from the point of view of a witness and it is an unadorned, clear and vivid image of the very moment when life expires. Dickinson familiarises the reader with Death by presenting a consequent realism of details.

> I've seen a Dying Eye
> Run round and round a Room –
> In search of Something – as it seemed –

Then Cloudier become –
And then – obscure with Fog –
And then – be soldered down
Without disclosing what it be
'T were blessed to have seen – (Dickinson 266)

The speaker seems emotionally detached and objective in her description. The stages of agony – movement of the eye, blurred vision and the final loss of eye contact with the world are delivered in a matter-of-fact manner and without any embellishment or glorification of death. Dickinson's realism is evident here in the revealing of the gruesome physical transformations that death brings.

The tendency to highlight details is also discernible in poem 71.

A throe upon the features –
A hurry in the breath –
An ecstasy of parting
Denominated "Death" – (Dickinson 37)

While the previously mentioned verse focuses on changes happening to vision, this poem shows different symptoms of approaching death. The words "throe," "ecstasy" and "breath" create a catalogue of features associated with dying. At first glance the word "ecstasy" seems out of place here, but it is justified when we think that the speaker may be bearing in mind God's promise of the Resurrection. Another explanation, following Kristeva, could be that in order to magnify Jesus' victimization, Christian tradition eroticized both pain and suffering (131). The physical dimension of this process is represented by an image of a spasm of pain and hurried breath. Once again to achieve realistic imagery the poet uses physiological terminology and defines bodily functions.

There cannot be a better way of getting the reader accustomed to the notion of death than to present it as a domestic ritual. Poem 158 stresses the intimacy of death. In this poem death is almost a daily activity and a home is its territory.

Dying! Dying in the night!
Won't somebody bring the light
So I can see which way to go
Into the everlasting snow? (Dickinson 74)

For the speaker death is nothing extraordinary. She is frightened because she is caught unprepared and uncertain about the road she should take, but the commands she gives betray her knowledge of the ritual. The realistic description of activities – bringing the light, inviting Jesus, opening the gate, present death in our earthly dimension, make it a "drama of departure" (St. Armand 54). The poetic practice of familiarising death is also shown by the presence of a close person who accompanies the dying instead of Christ.

> And "Jesus"! Where is *Jesus* gone?
> They said that Jesus – always came –
> Perhaps he doesn't know the House –
> This way, Jesus, Let him pass!
>
> Somebody run to the great gate
> And see if Dollie's coming! Wait!
> I hear her feet upon the stair!
> Death won't hurt – now Dollie's here! (Dickinson 74)

One can risk an interpretation that Dollie's visit is actually a visit of Christ. Such interpretation expresses a religious concept of the human body as a temple of God. If Christ comes as a real, ordinary human being, death stops being fearful and alien.

2.4. Conclusion: The functions of poetic techniques in Emily Dickinson's poems

Despite the strong intrusion of the semiotic into the symbolic the poet managed to gain control over her overpowering emotions and use them successfully as the subject matter of her poetry. Using Kristeva's theory four artistic techniques have been distinguished in Emily Dickinson's strategy of the portrayal of suffering: minimalism, composition of loneliness, irony and realism. Each of them, in different ways, shows that suffering is the dominant strategy of the poet's creative processes. These techniques also demonstrate that suffering in Dickinson's poetry is a theme as well as a form.

Conclusion

This analysis of a selection of Emily Dickinson's texts confirms the notion that suffering occupies the principal position in the poet's work. Her poetry constitutes an example of a painful literary quest for subjectivity as well as an act of self-transcendence, which means that through her writing the poet obtained conscious control over her personal anguish. By using pain as a poetic strategy she transformed her private biography into a literary text. In this way she became a model for coping with suffering and using it for self-examination and self-development.

In Emily Dickinson's poems suffering creates a new language and a new outlook on the self and the world. During the investigation of her poetic texts three dimensions of suffering as a poetic strategy have been distinguished: suffering as a theme, suffering as a subversive force affecting the language and suffering as a form of poetic expression. The critical tool used for this analysis was the theory of Julia Kristeva, who emphasises these elements as crucial in the interpretation of literary texts.

In Kristeva's theory the process of creation is a sublimation of "mourning" for the lost Thing: "the elusive preobject" (Kristeva 152), which should be understood as the indefinable source of contentment. Brutal separation from a mother's comfort leads to a constant quest for a satisfactory equivalent. The lack the subject feels becomes a source of creative expression. Following Julia Kristeva's concept that "'lack' is necessary for the *sign* to emerge" (Kristeva 23) the first chapter concentrated on Emily Dickinson's biographical deprivation and its metaphorisation in the texts. All her unruly feelings connected with the "lacks" of love, God and health found their way into the poems. Emotional turmoil and a life in isolation generated an impulse to examine her own inner life. The ability for penetrating self-observation resulted in the most profound portrayal of psychic processes. But introspection also became an effective way of confronting pain and discovering her own potential. The study revealed that through the astonishing poetic effort all the *lacks* were substituted with their satisfactory equivalent:

Lack of love – Adopting an unorthodox role for a woman
Lack of God – The new spirituality
Lack of health – Concept of immortality
Lack of independence – Constructive rage

By juxtaposing the contrary images of suffering the thesis presents an internal division of Dickinson's literary output. The first component is the profound characteristic of suffering resulting from deprivation. The second is its victorious conquest. Together they constitute a record of a successful process of mourning and a strategy of creation.

Examination of Emily Dickinson's poems in the light of Kristeva's theory of abjection has disclosed that the literary output of the poet is a congenial forerunner of some of the twentieth-century theories of subjectivity. Dickinson, in her verse, predates the findings of Julia Kristeva. This phenomenon classifies the poet as one of the precursors of twentieth-century philosophical thought, especially in the area of experimental poetic form and philosophical contemplation of subjectivity.

Another purpose of this thesis is to point to the poet's originality of language, which extends beyond the poetry of nineteenth-century romanticism. The application of Julia Kristeva's theory reveals that Emily Dickinson's poetry is characterised by the semiotic type of sensitivity. This conclusion has been drawn after discovering in the poet's language the full range of elements which Kristeva recognises as maternal energies namely: "unorderable cognitive chaos" (33), compression and elisions, unorthodox treatment of grammar, absurd phrases, slow delivery, repetitions and obsessive litanies, interruption in speech flows and mood swings. All these elements make the poet's work enigmatic and impenetrable. Interpretation is often reduced to hypothetical guesswork. Thus the most important finding of this work is that Emily Dickinson's poetry confirms Julia Kristeva's theory that the source of the poetic language is the process of mourning. Mourning denotes the practice through which the subject regains the lost Thing in speech. The lost Thing is always visible in the semiotic level of the language; that is in those elements which are unutterable or incoherent.

Grammar and structure of signification comprise the symbolic level of language. They are also evidence of a successful overcoming of mourning. To indicate the symbolic dimension of Emily Dickinson's poetic work we have analysed the following strategies: minimalism, composition, sarcasm and irony, and realism. They are an indication of the triumphant conquest of suffering and its use as a creative technique by the poet.

This thesis also stresses the practical dimension of Emily Dickinson's poetry. On account of her victorious self-transcendence, the poet's texts can be treated as a self-therapy project as well as a proposal to all those inflicted with pain. Emily Dickinson's poetry shows how to go beyond personal limitations and obtain a wider perspective of our true self. Anxiety and fear can be used as a chance to explore the most profound existential problems, such as one's own subjectivity, comprehension of love or experience of God. Suffering as a conflict – a process of discovering contradictions in the framework of one's own life – offers a new language of expression. Julia Kristeva emphasized that creative processes based on suffering change the depressive passivity of a subject (the semiotic dimension of language) into their creative potential (the symbolic element). The same notion can be found in Emily Dickinson's poetry that showed that healing is an inherent feature of creativity.

The healing power of Emily Dickinson's poetry lies in her presenting that suffering also has a positive, empowering side. By displaying an astounding autonomy and showing an alternative way of existence the poet demonstrated that fulfilment can be understood in a very broad sense. Her poetry constitutes evidence that the creative processes can be used as psychotherapy for both the creator and the recipient. Cindy MacKenzie and Barbara Dana have edited the book *Wider than the Sky*, which is "a collection of reminiscences, tributes and personal and scholarly essays" (xiv) written by people indebted to Emily Dickinson whose verse comforted them in sorrow. This book is the best evidence that Emily Dickinson's biggest dream – expressed in the poem below – came true.

If I can stop one Heart from breaking
I shall not live in vain
If I can ease one Life the Aching
Or cool one Pain

Or help one fainting Robin
Unto his Nest again
I shall not live in Vain (Dickinson 433).

Summary

The main purpose of this work is to analyse suffering as the theme and the strategy of the creative processes of Emily Dickinson. The analysis has been based on Julia Kristeva's theory of subjectivity. Her concept of the creative process points to two levels of the literary text. In Kristeva's terms the semiotic level corresponds to the depressive position of the subject, while the symbolic one to its overcoming through language. The semiotic level is characterised by those elements of speech which are preverbal, unutterable and connected with the experience of being a part of a mother's body. In Emily Dickinson's poetry the semiotic elements are responsible for making many fragments of her texts incomprehensible and hermetic. The symbolic level pertains to the denotative meanings of words, which render the texts easier for interpretation. This level, called by Kristeva "paternal," is a sign of conquering the inability for communication. It coordinates the language and is the textual sign of overcoming depression. It is this double dimension of the text that became central in analysing suffering as a poetic strategy in Emily Dickinson's poetic texts. According to Kristeva, during the act of creation, suffering and depressiveness are transformed into the conscious strategy of writing. In this way suffering can become the theme and the form of the poetic process. This transformation is the subject of a thorough analysis in this thesis. In Emily Dickinson's poetry lack – understood as an emotional deprivation – becomes the source of creativity. A private painful experience is changed into poetic metaphorisation. Emily Dickinson's poetry presents the Kristevan "subject in process" and its quest for subjectivity. The process of creation becomes the act of overcoming the destructive dimension of suffering and a conscious act of constructing the poetic language. The most important conclusion of this thesis is that suffering became for Emily Dickinson the act of poetic transgression. This transgression involved creating a new experimental poetic language. In this light Dickinson, the poet of a unique strategy of suffering, appears to be a precursor of some of the twentieth-century trends in poetry.

Streszczenie

Podstawowym celem pracy jest analiza cierpienia jako tematu i strategii aktu twórczego w poezji Emily Dickinson. Analiza i interpretacja twórczości poetki zostały dokonane na podstawie teorii podmiotowości sformułowanej przez Julię Kristevą. Wybór tej właśnie metodologii pracy uzasadnia koncepcja procesu twórczego Kristevej, której zastosowanie do poezji Dickinson obrazuje znaczenie dwu poziomów tekstu artystycznego. W terminologii Kristevej poziom semiotyczny tekstu odpowiada pozycji depresyjnej podmiotu, poziom symboliczny zaś pokonaniu tej deprywacji w porządku słownym języka. Semiotyczne jest tym, co przedsłowne, niewyrażalne i odnoszące się do doświadczenia człowieka z etapu bycia fragmentem ciała matczynego. W poezji Dickinson elementy semiotyczne wiążą się z niezrozumiałością (nieczytelnością) wielu fragmentów tekstu, z ich hermetycznością i niekomunikatywnym dyskursem depresji. Poziom symboliczny tekstu odnosi się do struktury słownej, komunikującej w możliwych do interpretacji znaczeniach. Ten poziom, zwany przez Kristevą ojcowskim, jest znakiem pokonania niemocy wyrażania. Wymiar symboliczny twórczości porządkuje jej odbiór, czyni możliwym do zrozumienia i staje się tekstowym znakiem pokonania depresji. Ten właśnie schemat odpowiada procesowi cierpienia jako poetyckiej teorii aktu twórczego w poezji Dickinson. Cierpienie i depresyjność podmiotu poetyckiego zostają przekształcone przez poetkę w świadomą strategię pisania i w ten sposób cierpienie może się stać tematem i formą procesu poetyckiego. W niniejszej pracy dogłębnej analizie została poddana powyższa zasada transformacji emocjonalnego braku w poetycki sposób metaforyzacji tego doświadczenia. Innymi słowy: w twórczości Dickinson odkrywamy specyficzną technikę ekspresji podmiotu. W poezji Emily Dickinson brak staje się źródłem rozbudowanej metafory. Metafora pozwala uchwycić w analizie poezji Dickinson poetycką strategię budowania tożsamości podmiotu aktu twórczego. Strategia ta stanowi proces pokonywania destrukcyjnego wymiaru cierpienia i świadomy akt tworzenia języka poetyckiego. A zatem główną konkluzją diagnozy, analizy i interpretacji poezji Emily Dickinson zaprezentowaną w pracy jest wykazanie, że cierpienie to dla poetki akt poetyckiej transgresji. Owa transgresja polega na procesie kreacji nowatorskiego, eksperymentalnego języka poetyckiego. W tym świetle Dickinson, poetka unikalnej strategii cierpienia, jawi się jako prekursorka niektórych dwudziestowiecznych nurtów poezji.

Works Cited

Bennett, Paula. *Emily Dickinson: Woman Poet.* Iowa City: University of Iowa Press, 1990.

Cody, John. *After Great Pain: The Inner Life of Emily Dickinson*. Cambridge, Massachusetts: The Belknap Press Harvard University Press, 1971.

Conrad, Angela. *The Wayward Nun of Amherst: Emily Dickinson and Medieval Mystical Women.* New York: Garland Publishing, 2000.

Dickinson, Emily. *Letters of Emily Dickinson.* Ed. Mabel Loomis Todd, New York: Dover Publication, 2003.

Doll, Mary Aswell, Delese Wear and Martha L. Whitaker. *Triple Takes on Curricular Worlds.* Albany: State University of New York Press, 2006.

Doriani, Beth Maclay. *Emily Dickinson, Daughter of Prophecy.* Boston: The University of Massachusetts Press, 1996.

Farr, Judith. *The Passion of Emily Dickinson*. Cambridge, Massachusetts: Harvard University Press, 1992.

French, Patrick, and Roland-.François Lack, eds. *The Tel Quel Reader.* London: Routledge, 1998.

Gabora, Liane, and Nancy Holmes. "Dangling from a Tassel on the Fabric of Socially Constructed Reality: Reflections on the Creative Writing Process." *The Dark Side of Creativity*. Ed. David H. Cropley et al. Cambridge: Cambridge University Press, 2010, 277–296.

Grabher, Gurdun, Roland Hagenbüchle, and Cristanne Miller, eds. *The Emily Dickinson Handbook.* Boston: The University of Massachusetts Press, 1998.

Guthrie, James R. *Emily Dickinson's Vision: Illness and Identity in Her Poetry.* Gainesville: University Press of Florida, 1998.

Hogue, Cynthia. *Scheming Women: Poetry, Privilege, and the Politics of Subjectivity.* Albany: State University of New York, 1995.

Johnson, Thomas Herbert, ed. The *Complete Poems of Emily Dickinson.* Cambridge, Massachusetts: Harvard University Press, 1960.

Kameen, Paul. *Writing/Teaching: Essays Toward a Rhetoric of Pedagogy.* Pittsburgh: University of Pittsburgh Press, 2000.

Keane, Patrick J. *Emily Dickinson's Approving God: Divine Design and the Problem of Suffering.* Columbia, Missouri: University of Missouri Press, 2008.

Kristeva, Julia. *Black Sun: Depression and Melancholia.* From French translated by Roudiez L.S. New York: Columbia University Press, 1989.

Leiter, Sharon. *Critical Companion to Emily Dickinson: a Literary Reference to Her Life and Work.* New York: Facts on File, Inc., 2007.

Lundin, Roger. *Emily Dickinson and The Art of Belief.* 2nd ed. Cambridge: Wm. B. Eerdmans Publishing Co, 2004.
McAfee, Noëlle. *Julia Kristeva.* New York: Routledge, 2004.
MacKenzie, Cindy and Dana Barbara. *Wider than the Sky: Essays and Meditation on the Healing Power of Emily Dickinson.* Kent, Ohio: The Kent State University Press, 2007.
McDermott, John F. "Emily Dickinson Revisited: A Study of Periodicity in Her Work." *American Journal of Psychiatry* 158 (2001): 686–690.
McIntosh, James. *Nimble Believing: Dickinson and the Unknown.* USA: The University of Michigan Press, 2004.
Mamunes, George. *"So Has a Daisy Vanished": Emily Dickinson and Tuberculosis.* Jefferson, North Carolina: McFarland and Company, 2007.
Martin, Wendy. *An American Triptych: Anne Bradstreet, Emily Dickinson, Adrienne Rich.* USA: The University of North Carolina Press, 1984.
Martin, Wendy. *The Cambridge Introduction to Emily Dickinson.* New York: Cambridge University Press, 2007.
Miller, Cristanne. *Emily Dickinson: A Poet's Grammar.* Cambridge, Massachusetts: Harvard University Press, 1987.
Mills, Jon, ed. *Rereading Freud: Psychoanalysis through Philosophy.* Albany: State University of New York Press, 2004.
Niall, Lucy. *Postmodern Literary Theory: an Anthology.* Oxford: Blackwell Publishers, 2000.
Oliver, Kelly. *Family Values: Subjects Between Nature and Culture.* London: Routledge, 1997.
Orzeck, Martin, and Robert Weisbuch, eds. *Dickinson and Audience.* USA: The University of Michigan Press, 1996.
Petrino, Elizabeth A. *Emily Dickinson and her Contemporaries: Women's Verse in America, 1820–1885.* Hanover, Hew Hampshire: University Press of New England, 1998.
Phillips, Elizabeth. *Emily Dickinson: Personae and Performance.* USA: Pennsylvania State University Press, 1988.
Pollack, Vivian R., ed. *A Historical Guide to Emily Dickinson.* USA: Oxford University Press, 2004.
Porter, David T. *Dickinson, the modern idiom.* Cambridge, Massachusetts: Harvard University Press, 1981.
Priddy, Anna. *Bloom's How to Write about Emily Dickinson.* New York: Bloom's Literary Criticism, 2008.
Ritzer, George, ed. *Encyclopedia of Social Theory, Volume 1.* California: Sage Publications, 2005.
Rutledge, David. "Dickinson's I know that he exists." *Explicator* 52.2 (1994): 81–83.
St. Armand, Barton Levi. *Emily Dickinson and Her Culture.* New York: Cambridge University Press, 1984.
Scheurich, Neil. "Suffering and Spirituality in the Poetry of Emily Dickinson." *Pastoral Psychology* 56.2 (2007): 189–197. *Academic Search Complete.* EBSCO Publishing. 2 Aug. 2010.

<http://search.ebscohost.com/login.aspx?direct=true&db=a9h&AN=27322382&site=ehost-live">

Sewall, Richard B. *The Life of Emily Dickinson.* Cambridge, Massachusetts: Harvard University Press, 1994.

Sielke, Sabine. *Fashioning the Female Subject: The Intertextual Networking of Dickinson, Moore and Rich.* USA: The University of Michigan Press, 1997.

Small, Judy Jo. *Positive as Sound: Emily Dickinson's Rhyme.* Athens, Georgia: University of Georgia Press, 1990.

Smith, Anne-Marie. *Julia Kristeva: Speaking the Unspeakable.* London: Pluto Press, 1998.

Smith, Martha Nell. *Rowing in Eden: Rereading Emily Dickinson.* Austin, Texas: University of Texas Press, 1992.

Stiles, Bradley J. *Emerson's Contemporaries and Kerouac's Crowd: A Problem of Self-Location.* London: Associated University Presses, 2003.

Tandon, Neeru and Anjana Trevedi, Thematic *Patterns Of Emily Dickinson's Poetry.* New Delhi: Atlantic, 2008.

van Peer, Willie. *The Quality of Literature: Linguistic Studies in Literary Evaluation.* Amsterdam: John Benjamins Publishing Company, 2008.

Vendler, Helen. *Dickinson: Selected Poems and Commentaries.* Cambridge, Massachusetts: Harvard University Press, 2010.

Vendler, Helen. *Poets Thinking: Pope, Whitman, Dickinson, Yeats.* Cambridge, Massachusetts: Harvard University Press, 2006.

White, Fred D. *Approaching Emily Dickinson: Critical Currents and Crosscurrents Since 1960.* New York: Camden House, 2008.

Wolff, G. Griffin. *Emily Dickinson.* New York: Alfred A. Knopf, 1987.

Copy-editor
Tony Ames

Technical editors
Jadwiga Makowiec
Jerzy Hrycyk

Typesetter
Katarzyna Mróz-Jaskuła

Jagiellonian University Press
Editorial Offices:
Michałowskiego St. 9/2, 31-126 Cracow
Phone: +48 12 631 18 81, +48 12 631 18 82, Fax: +48 12 631 18 83

Writing Life